JOE BARB
A BUSINE

That's how Joe has always looked upon himself. When he beat a man to a bloody pulp, it was business. When he set up a man for a hit, it was business. When he shot a man down on the street or in his home, it was business. Now Joe Barboza opens his books—in a thorough accounting of all the business he did during his years of bloodletting in the underworld. There is no apology in his voice or regret or even embarrassment as he details the most gruesome aspects of his trade. There is just the calm tone and special language of a professional talking about his work. It will shock you as nothing you have ever read before.

BOOKS BY HANK MESSICK AVAILABLE FROM
COMMONWEALTH BOOK COMPANY

Syndicate Wife: The Story of Ann Drahmann Coppola

The Silent Syndicate

Syndicate in the Sun

Syndicate Abroad

Razzle Dazzle

BARBOZA

JOE
BARBOZA
WITH
HANK MESSICK

COMMONWEALTH BOOK COMPANY
ST. MARTIN, OHIO

To Edward F. Harrington,
With Respect

Woe to they, the very few, who
will always be alone.

> From an unpublished poem
> by Joe Barboza

Who is worse, the fellow who
opens doors for killers, or the
one who kills?

> U. S. Attorney Paul Markham,
> United States v. Patriarca

Did He who made the lamb make thee?

> William Blake

Coauthor's Note

Basically this is Joe Barboza's book, but Joe is a fighter, not a writer. I've taken his words and rearranged them for clarity without sacrificing either his language or his meaning. Independently, I've tried to put Joe and his jungle into perspective. However, the reader will have no difficulty in determining where Messick ends and Barboza begins.

Many people on both sides of the law have contributed to my understanding of Joe and of the events in Boston with which he was involved. Not all can be named and none bear any responsibility for the contents of this book. Specifically I would thank Dennis Condon, Paul Rico and Bob Sheehan of the FBI; John Doyle, chief investigator for District Attorney Garrett Byrne; Paul Markham, now a private attorney in Boston; and, most important, Margaret Delfel, a charming citizen of San Francisco.

In addition I should mention those several potential authors who for personal reasons left the writing of this book to me. Thanks, fellows, and keep watching for things that go bump in the night.

Hank Messick
Peace River, Arcadia, Florida, 1975

Contents

Prologue

Mankiller

I was sitting in the Roman Gardens restaurant with Henry Tameleo. We were eating calamares and talking about Jackie Nazzarin.

Henry ran things in Boston for the Office. Jackie had been a top gun for the Office and he won his fame when he killed Tiger Baletto, an ex-fighter who was real good with his fists. Jackie was real good with a gun. New York borrowed him for awhile and he was one of the two men who killed Albert Anastasia in that barbershop. It gave him ideas. He came back to Boston and began talking too much.

When we finished the calamares, Henry and I walked back into the lounge section of the restaurant. Henry pointed to a corner and said: "He was sitting right there drinking. He had a bottle in his hand and he was drunk. They had sent for me to try to talk him out of it. I tried. I began talking to him. He didn't listen.

"'Fuck you,' Jackie said to me. 'Fuck all of you. I'm taking over the Office.'

"I calmed him down and took him home. He was of no use to us anymore. Uncontrollable."

Jackie was shot down in broad daylight a little later. The killer was arrested.

"It cost us over a hundred thousand to beat that case," Henry said. "I was at the lawyer's office every night for a month preparing the witnesses. One asshole had just a few lines to say but I had to work with him for fifteen nights to get him to say them straight."

There was a long pause. Then I said: "Henry, I heard Nazzarin killed roughly twenty-six people for the Office."

Henry looked off into the distance and spoke softly: "Yes, he was a good man gone bad, but in this business everybody dies."

Part I

The Jungle

Salisbury Beach is a resort town north of Boston near the New Hampshire line. Its nightclubs once featured top show business stars up front, and casinos in the back that paid their fees. Among the visitors in September, 1961, were three couples who moved into the upstairs of a rental house and proceeded to get stinking drunk. Georgie McLaughlin, a five-foot three inch psychopath, was there with a pretty friend. The other men were Red Lloyd and Billy Hickey, both of Somerville near Boston. With them were their current broads. The word is used advisedly.

McLaughlin was the man who expected respect. With his brothers, Bernie and Punchie, he was an independent operator who had been retained on occasion to kill for the Office—as the local Mafia family was known. One particular episode was talked about with mixed emotions. Georgie was about to fire the fatal shot and earn his pay when the victim suddenly asked if he could have a minute to pray. Georgie said okay. The victim got on his knees and prayed. When his minute was up Georgie shot him in the back of the head and spit on the body. "You weak son of a bitch," he said, and walked away.

Lloyd and Hickey worked with the McLaughlin occasionally, but they kept a wary eye on Georgie. The more

Georgie drank the more nervous they became. About 6 A.M., after a night of booze and sex, they persuaded Georgie to go for a swim in the Atlantic. He came back still drunk. All night long he had been eyeing Ann. She was Lloyd's girl and she had breasts so large they were freaky. Lloyd didn't care for her personally since he considered her something of a pig, but, still, she was with him and, in a sense, his property. So when Georgie reached out to cup those huge breasts, Lloyd just had to object.

Nothing much happened then since Georgie didn't actually touch Ann. The women decided they needed some sleep. The men went out into the kitchen for another drink and that's where the fight began. Georgie made some remarks about Ann and Lloyd slugged him. Lloyd got scared then. So did Hickey who joined in. Together, the two men beat the sodden McLaughlin into unconsciousness. In fact, they didn't stop until they thought Georgie was dead. Knowing how his brothers would react to that, they loaded the body into a car and drove off to find a lonely spot to dump it. But Georgie was too tough to die. Suddenly he regained consciousness and stuck his battered face out of the back window.

Lloyd and Hickey made a quick decision. They drove to the hospital and dropped McLaughlin on the lawn. Then they got out of town fast, stopping at home only long enough to pack their suitcases.

Next day Bernie McLaughlin went looking for the men who had beaten his brother. When he couldn't find them after a couple of weeks, he went to the home of James "Buddy" McLean. Buddy, a husky six-footer, was known to be a good friend of the missing men. Of German extraction but brought up by foster parents of Portuguese descent, McLean was well liked and respected by the diverse criminal elements of the Boston area. He was known as a straight shooter who lived by a code and always laid his cards on the table.

It was because people trusted McLean that McLaughlin

made his request.

"Buddy," he said, "I want you to help me set up these guys that beat up Georgie."

Buddy replied: "Listen, I'm friends with you and I'm friends with those guys. I don't set up my friends."

Bernie seemed astonished. "You're still friends with those motherfuckers after what they did to Georgie?"

"From what I hear, Georgie was way out of line," McLean said coldly. "I don't want to get involved."

"Whatta you mean?" demanded McLaughlin. "I'm making you involved. You're either with them or with us."

"Your threats don't scare me," said the modern-day Ivan Skavar. "I'm not helping you set up my friends."

Without a word, Bernie McLaughlin got up and walked out of the house.

Several September days passed and then one night barking dogs aroused McLean's wife from sleep. She looked from the window and saw three men doing something to the McLean automobile parked below on the street. She alerted her husband who grabbed his Luger and slipped out of the house in his undershorts. From behind a bush he opened fire. The shadowy figures fired back, then ran down the street to a waiting car. McLean recognized Bernie McLaughlin as one of them. Beneath his car he found five sticks of dynamite wired to the ignition switch.

As McLean told it later, he removed the dynamite, went back into the house and sat down until his body stopped trembling. For he knew that—barring a miracle—the booby-trapped car would have killed his wife and children. Each morning his wife used the car first to take the kids to school.

To attempt to kill a man for refusing to betray his friends was bad enough, but to risk blasting an innocent mother and her children was unforgivable. McLean's code demanded a quick reply.

Bernie McLaughlin was gunned down at high noon

next day as he walked in front of the police station on the public square in the Boston district of Charlestown. Trains rumbled along the elevated tracks and an estimated one hundred persons watched as McLean killed McLaughlin with a shotgun blast. Yet a grand jury refused to indict on the grounds there were no witnesses willing to talk.

McLean, however, was sent to prison on another charge. For two years the surviving McLaughlins waited. The FBI was to claim later that the murder of George Joynt in July, 1962, was a result of the feud, but it wasn't until March, 1964, that the bade was joined in earnest. Sixteen killings in that year were attributed to the gang war, and it was but the beginning.

In the excitement, Red Lloyd and Billy Hickey—the men who had beaten Georgie McLaughlin for "insulting" a prostitute—were forgotten.

It was this slaughter of more than forty men over a three-year period that finally brought Boston and the New England area a measure of national attention. Thanks to corrupt officials who made no honest investigations and a largely compliant press more interested in politics than public service, the gangsters had been able to operate without publicity. The Kefauver Committee in 1950–51 took note of the situation but bypassed an intensive probe in favor of areas that had more responsive newspaper coverage. When in 1963, Joseph Valachi made mention of Raymond Patriarca in privileged testimony, the *Boston Herald* thought it deserved high praise for daring to do what most other papers in the country outside of Boston did as a matter of routine—report the news. Patriarca, when he recovered from the shock, promptly sued in a successful effort to discourage any future outbreak of journalistic enterprise.

Thanks at least in part to the absence of the spotlight, multi-ethnic gangs and gangsters thrived in Massachusetts in general and Boston in particular. In perhaps no other city, not excepting Chicago, was the alliance between crime and politics so strong and so little concealed. Mayor James M. Curley became a legend and his ultimate conviction on federal charges of mail fraud did little to diminish his power. Moreover, Curley was typical rather than unique as far as public morality was concerned. His political strength was based on the Irish population which in the latter part of the 19th century had flooded into Boston in such numbers as to ultimately outvote the pioneer Yankees. Jews from Eastern Europe followed and then a tidal wave of Italians. Boston developed into a city of sharply defined ghettos: Jewish, Irish, Italian, Negro and even Chinese. Other national groups formed islands of their own: Portuguese, Syrian, Greek and German. Moreover, there was little commingling. The fabled "melting pot" didn't work.

Crime in New England as elsewhere got its biggest push with Prohibition. The long shoreline offered rum runners, large and small, ample opportunity and, certainly, the reputation of the Irish as heavy drinkers didn't suffer. A "rum row" existed off Boston harbor as it did off New York, New Orleans and San Francisco. Liquor brought in legally from Canada, the Bahamas and England was unloaded into small boats which ran it ashore under cover of darkness. The "Big Seven," an organization of bootleggers put together in New York by Johnny Torrio and Meyer Lansky, included a representative from Boston—Charles "King" Solomon. Among his lieutenants who survived his untimely death in 1933, were such notables as Joseph Linsey, Hyman Abrams and Louis Fox. In years to come, Linsey would become a "philanthropist" and part owner of horse and dog tracks, liquor stores and country clubs. Abrams would become an important figure in Las Vegas, and Fox would boss the resort town of Revere. To young punks coming along, such men as Linsey and Abrams would become increasingly remote until such a person as Joe Barboza could assume they were but front men for the better known Patriarca. Needless to add, such attitudes were encouraged by the elder statesmen who knew the value of anonymity and by the younger executives who, in reality, fronted for them in violent crime.

The bootleggers made a lot of money in Boston as elsewhere and, when the era ended, they turned to gambling. The old alliances still served as was illustrated when an Internal Revenue Service probe of dog racing tied Abrams, Fox and others to State Representative Martin Hays. All were indicted and convicted on various counts of bribery and corruption, and all received suspended sentences and fines. Throughout the years that followed, racing scandals broke at infrequent intervals, but nothing effective was done to eliminate Mob influence. Casino gambling flourished in Revere and in Boston proper. A huge numbers racket developed and became part of the way of life for thousands of citizens. The winning number was based in time on the parimutuel "handle" at various dog and horse tracks, and Boston newspapers carried the necessary information on the front page of their "Payoff Edition."

The Mafia as an organization has a long history in Boston, but at no time did it have anything approaching control. As elsewhere it was brought over by Sicilians and in its early days it preyed largely on persons of Sicilian and Italian extraction. During the easy money of Prohibition it gained in strength as King Solomon and his successors gave employment to Mafia members. During the great Masseria-Maranzano war, an internal power struggle, a "Grand Council" of the Mafia met in Boston. The site was selected because Gaspare Messina, *Capo* of Boston, had just been elected the provisional *Capo di Capi Re* of the Mafia in the United States. He would hold the title until one side or the other won the civil war so, meanwhile, protocol dictated the Grand Council meet in his city. At the convention—and that's what the session really was—a committee was appointed to try to mediate the dispute. It failed. Ultimately a group of "Young Americans" headed by Charles Luciano settled the matter by killing Masseria. When Maranzano proved a worse tyrant, Luciano called on his allies, the Bugs and Meyer Mob, to knock off the new dictator. The Mafia remained a fragmented, largely autonomous organization, whose power varied from city to city, but Luciano made it a part of the emerging national "combination" which evolved at the end of Prohibition.

Frank "Butsy" Morelli succeeded as head of the Mafia *borgate*, or family, which had limited authority through much of New England. Morelli, however, made his headquarters in Providence, Rhode Island, following the theory expounded by Johnny Torrio that it is cheaper to corrupt a small city than a large one. Morelli had no particular difficulty with the law until in 1948 he gave shelter to "Trigger Mike" Coppola's wife and father-in-law. New York officials wanted to question them in the sensational murder of Joseph Scottoriggio in New York. By the time the district attorney's men discovered their hiding place, the fugitives had fled to Florida. Morelli was questioned by a grand jury and he talked. When this became apparent, Morelli was finished. His place was taken by Raymond L. S. Patriarca, also of Providence.

Patriarca had served an apprenticeship in prison for armed robbery, but it was a short one. Sentenced to a three to five year term in 1938, he was pardoned eighty-four days later. The scandal caused the impeachment of Massachusetts Governor's Councillor Daniel Coakley who had personally drafted the pardon petition which pictured Raymond as a virtuous youth anxious to go home to his aged mother. The record showed Patriarca did go home but only for a change of clothing. He then departed with a blonde to Miami Beach.

During Patriarca's tenure he was plagued by a shortage of manpower. Once the elite of the "Italian Mob"—to use a term favored by the FBI prior to Valachi—the Mafia now consisted of a handful of elderly men who saw no need to take unnecessary chances. Second and third generation

Americans were no longer willing to submit to the old-world discipline of a *capo*. The mumbo jumbo of blood oaths and codes of silence which had once bound uneducated immigrants was as outdated as the Black Hand. The Mafia was dying and in another generation would be little more than a bad memory.

Patriarca, nevertheless, used his resources wisely. Money and guile were his weapons. Unable to recruit young members who to prove their dedication would be willing to kill, he turned to ambitious youths from other ethnic groups. The "Office," as the Mafia was called, had prestige because no other group had developed modern leaders about which to unite. So an unscrupulous and perhaps not too well-informed young man was sometimes willing to take pay and, he assumed, goodwill, for performing as a Mafia mercenary. Such hired enforcers were used not only to stomp on outsiders who might cause problems, but to keep Mafia members themselves in line. Patriarca chose his proteges carefully, tried to buy their allegiance, and double-crossed them when it became expedient to do so. "To meet the man" became a goal, and it was not achieved until the prospect proved his worth by a well-executed murder.

On December 1, 1966, the FBI prepared a report on *La Cosa Nostra* as it stubbornly persisted in calling the Mafia. The report was concerned with the states of Massachusetts, Maine, New Hampshire and Rhode Island, the area comprising the FBI's Boston division. It noted that Patriarca "controls all. LCN membership in this division with the possible exception of Worcester and Springfield, Massachusetts." That area was said to be controlled by Samuel "Big Nose" Cufari, a *capo decina* in a New York family of LCN.

According to the FBI report: "At the present time there are fifty known members of the LCN in this division. Thirteen of these members are in Providence, Rhode Island; seven in Worcester, Massachusetts; four in Springfield, Massachusetts;

twenty-five in Boston, Massachusetts; and one in Portland, Maine."

Patriarca, therefore, according to the FBI, bossed thirty-nine men—if the eleven in Worcester and Springfield are subtracted. Yet thirteen months after the FBI report was issued, Attorney General Elliott L. Richardson estimated there were "5,000 members of organized crime in Massachusetts" alone. Surely then, if the FBI was right in saying Patriarca was "the policymaker, judge and overlord of organized crime in this area," it was a classic case of the tail wagging the dog.

The FBI had its private reasons for assigning such power to Patriarca, but the legend couldn't have been perpetuated had Boston possessed an enterprising and objective newspaper. The fact that old bootlegger, Joe Linsey, was a part owner of The *Boston Herald* may have had something, to do with that particular newspaper's failure, but it doesn't explain why other papers ignored their responsibility.

According to that 1966 FBI report, the *capo decina*—literally, it means "head of ten"—in the district controlled by Patriarca were Gennaro (Jerry) Anguilo, Joseph Anselmo, Michael Rocco, Henry Tameleo and Chester Iacone. Joseph Lombardo was listed as *consiglieri* or counselor of the "family."

Of these men, Rocco was perhaps the most unique. Like the others, a veteran, Rocco was known popularly as "Mickey the Wise Guy." In a general way, the term "wise guy" came to be synonymous with Mafia membership among the thousands of not always respectful non-Mafia gangsters. Mickey, however, had respect. He was the Mafia's liaison with the National Crime Syndicate. Any Mafia member wanting to discuss a business venture with the syndicate had to get approval of his *capo decina* and of Patriarca. The *capo* would then ask Rocco to discuss the matter with Linsey. Rocco occupied much the same position with Linsey as Vincent "Jimmy Blue Eyes" Alo did with Meyer Lansky. Perhaps to facilitate matters, and to explain the relationship, Rocco was officially employed by two of Linsey's companies, an automobile agency and a liquor company. Basically, however, Rocco was concerned with running the numbers racket in East Boston.

But the syndicate was concerned with national and international projects. The old-fashioned rackets: minor shylocking, extortion, barbut games, race-fixing and the like were crumbs left for local consumption. They provided income for the organized minority that was the Mafia, and for the thousands of independents. One such individual was Joe Barboza who liked to refer to himself as a "Portugee from New Bedford."

Barboza's parents were married in 1927. His father was a native of Fall River, Massachusetts, and his mother hailed from New Bedford. Their parents had been born in Portugal. At the time of their marriage the textile business was booming in New England, but change was at hand. When Joseph Barboza, Jr.—the second child—was born on September 20, 1932, economic depression lay heavy on the land. With steady work hard to find, the father turned to professional boxing. It brought in a few dollars but no security.

The marriage seems to have gone sour almost from the beginning. The father was handsome and restless. The mother sought to bind him to her with children, ignoring as best she could his affairs with other women. As the son wrote much later: "The house we lived in was more of sorrow than of happiness. We were constantly on welfare. My mother was very much in love with my father regardless of his infidelities, and took out her loneliness by constantly keeping my brother and I around her. But both of us were wild."

At one point the boys came home to find their mother unconscious with the gas jet open. They blamed their father but at the same time they worshipped him. Disillusion for young Joe came, however, when his mother sent him to beg his father to leave the woman he was shacked up with and return home. As Joe has told it: "My mother waited down the street and sent me to get my father. He was in the yard with Cecilia. I told him I wanted to see him. He looked at me with anger in his eyes and said: 'Get out of here, you little bastard.' I turned around blindly and ran down the street. I couldn't stop crying. He came after me in his car as I reached my mother. She told my father triumphantly: 'He will never forget this.' I cried all the way home. I couldn't stop. He bought me a pigeon to pacify me. I've thought of this many times. The punk broke my heart."

Sensing that his mother was using him "to keep what little she had of my father," Joe turned to the streets where "I felt a better type of love." Responding to his aggressiveness, a gang of boys developed around him. From shoplifting they soon graduated to breaking-and-entering. While they knew the value of merchandise that could be fenced for cash, they remained boys. More than once a break-in was inspired by windowshopping earlier in the day. If they saw something they wanted, they came back that night to get it.

At age fourteen he was sent to Lyman Reform School. Today he remembers it as a "hellhole" where brutality was the rule rather than the exception. He was beaten many times and saw other boys beaten with everything from belts to pick handles. A special punishment known as the "hot foot" consisted of blows to the arch of the naked foot. One had to be tough to survive Lyman with spirit unbroken, and Joe Barboza was tough. He served three terms in the school, had more than three hundred fights and emerged as the undisputed champion. Logically enough, he began to think of fighting as a career. Involved also, perhaps, was a desire to impress and surpass his father.

The preliminary to a professional career was a good record as an amateur. Joe was too young, but he solved the problem by using someone else's birth certificate. Under these false colors he won eighteen of twenty fights and attracted the attention ultimately of professional managers who would pull strings to get him out of prison on parole.

Barboza's gang continued its nocturnal activities, occasionally mixing business with pleasure. When an instructor at a vocational school that Joe was briefly attending insulted him in woodworking class, the gang broke into his house and "trashed" it. The place was literally torn apart and even a cream pie was left dripping from the wall. Thereafter, the gang was known to police as "the Cream Pie Bandits" and every break-in not otherwise attributable was blamed on it.

Eventually arrested, Barboza made the front page of his hometown newspaper on the day he was sentenced to five years and a day in the Massachusetts Reformatory at Concord. On February 9, 1950, he entered prison. He was 17 years old. From the waist up he looked like a heavyweight, but his legs were short. Darkly handsome like his father, he nevertheless possessed an almost romantic attitude toward women. Long years in prison, formative years, were to deny him the associations that might have changed his mind. In maturity he could excuse a man who killed but he had complete contempt for anyone who mistreated a woman. And even today his love life remains very much his personal business about which he does not speak.

Upon entering Concord he worked first in a weaving mill and then was assigned to a dining room. There he had a fight with an older man. A left hook to the jaw broke the man's jaw in two places and got the victor nine days in solitary. Upon getting out he was assigned to shovel coal in the boiler room, perhaps in the belief he needed physical exercise as an outlet for his aggressiveness. In January, 1951, he was transferred to the Norfolk Prison Colony, supposedly a rehabilitation center. There he began boxing as a middleweight, knocking out older men as a matter of routine. Still he had energy left over to get into trouble. The climax came in September when he became high from sniffing paint thinner and challenged the guards to come and get him. For two hours a stalemate existed, but the "high" evaporated and Joe negotiated peace terms. He was sent back to Concord as a result—at 19 considered beyond rehabilitation.

Joe was growing in several ways. He was now a light-heavyweight, and won the prison championship in that division by beating Walter "Rocky" Stone. Moreover, he was able to "move" a guard into bringing in benny pills, liquor, knives and food for sale to the inmates. A man had to be a good fighter to protect such valuables from thieves. Perhaps recognizing that Barboza had dangerous leadership potential, the warden promised he could work at the prison farm if he behaved himself. Despite this bribe offer, Barboza took part in a prison riot. He spent eight days on bread and water and thirty more days in solitary for his role in the outbreak. Only then did he get to go to the farm, the warden obviously concluding he could cause less trouble there.

Driving a team of horses was a new experience for the youth, and he "dug it" very much. Other things were nice too. As he put it: "I really enjoyed the farm. I would sneak up the hill to a water reservoir and swim. I used to steal chickens from the prison hen house, have them plucked in the farm boiler room, and have a convict in the kitchen fry them. I watched TV every night."

Barboza was promised that the "good time" ordinarily subtracted from his sentence but lost as a result of the riot, would be restored if he behaved himself. As happened often with Barboza and his colleagues, he concentrated on avoiding detection. Every man is well-behaved until caught, was his theory. Unfortunately, he was betrayed by homebrew one night when he had only three months to go. With several friends he was sitting in the boiler room drinking. One asshole, as he put it, got carried away and began acting suspiciously. From the actions of the guards, Joe concluded the game was up. Next day, he decided, he would be returned to the main prison with his "good time" gone once more. One has to assume that he was pretty drunk. In any event he talked some of his fellow drunks into escaping. They locked up the guards, stole an ancient car belonging to one of them, and drove off down the hill.

It was a very short vacation. The car conked out, so they stole another one. Barboza hit a man who tried to interfere, fracturing his cheekbone. Next day in Revere he was picked up. At the police station he had a fight with a photographer. An investigation into prison conditions was begun after other prisoners reported that Barboza had an arrangement with certain guards to bring in contraband.

Meanwhile, Barboza was again in solitary. A guard came to see him. Words were exchanged. Joe hit the guard with a table. Six guards rushed in to rescue their fellow guard and all were needed to hog-tie the prisoner and hustle him into a dungeon where he spent the next ten days on bread and water. Even so, he refused to testify against the guards despite promises of light punishment. As a result he was given a new sentence of from ten to twelve years to be served at the old Charlestown State Prison. It was April, 1954.

The old prison looked like a fortress. Its walls were built of huge slabs of granite. Dust from the railroad coal yards just outside the prison covered the walls and the interior with a clinging gray film. The cells had no plumbing. Each cell was equipped with a toilet bucket, a pitcher of water and a basin in which to wash. The prisoners ate their meals in the cells, from trays wheeled around on carts. Every conceivable method of escape from the "Gray Monster" had been tried, and despite repeated failures would be tried again. The year before a serious riot had occurred when inmates used guns hidden in the prison earlier by a man who believed in looking ahead. The attempt failed but not all of the guns were found by authorities. Some months after Barboza arrived, a new attempt was made. The hardened prisoners segregated in the

Cherry Hill section of the prison took their guards hostage and attempted to bargain for their liberty. A siege began that lasted for eighty-five hours, Tanks were used. Ultimately the revolt was crushed, but the publicity brought demands for reform and hastened the construction of Walpole State Prison. When it was completed the old prison was torn down.

Barboza was moved to Walpole where reform-minded prison officials won his cooperation and respect. Perhaps Joe realized that it was time to really start behaving if he expected to ever go free. As a reward, he was returned to the Norfolk Prison Colony, and in June, 1958, he at last was paroled. He had been in prison for more than eight years. He was to remain out for three months.

It was a busy summer. Turning professional, Barboza had three fights, winning two of them. He also found and married an East Boston divorcee. She was sixteen years older than Joe and had four children to support. When in September he was returned to Walpole on a three-to-five, she divorced him. For Barboza, it perhaps represented the final break with his mother.

The world moved on. While this grandson of immigrants was completing his prison education and preparing to move into the public eye, another young man more fortunate in his parents was seeking the Democratic nomination for president of the United States. Massachusetts' favorite son would win that nomination in 1960 and go on to defeat Richard M. Nixon the following November. As loyal to his family as Bernie McLaughlin, he would appoint his brother attorney general to lead a coordinated war on organized crime. Eventually that war would give Joe Barboza a chance to gain a measure of revenge against a society which trapped him in prison while John F. Kennedy prepared for "Camelot."

Long before that chance developed, however, the multi-ethnic underworld of Boston ignored the protests of the Mafia and cheerfully engaged in the biggest gang war since

Salvatore Maranzano challenged Joe "the Boss" Masseria.

It was perhaps inevitable that a man born to trouble, such as Barboza, would become involved—if he could ever get out of jail long enough.

Part II

On the Prowl

1

The Hunter

After spending years in various prisons, Joe Barboza was eager to begin emulating the tough guys he had heard so much about. It was time to begin the hunt.

1

When I went back to Walpole in September, 1958, the warden called me into his office and said he'd put me outside the walls to work if I'd behave myself for a few months. It was a bribe and I figured it was worth taking.

Because of all my kitchen experience, I was made kitchen manager and runner. My job was to make out the weekly menus, get guys to work in the kitchen and pass food in the chow line. The warden figured I could handle all the troublemakers and cuckoos, so I had them all out in the kitchen. There was Blimp Lewis, Charley Cantofanti, John Amaral and Eddie Kilrow. It was this weasel Kilrow that kept giving me a bad time so one day I decided I'd better do something about it.

One day Blimp was talking to Kilrow in the back vegetable room. I had Amaral and Cantofanti keep the peep. When the lines started through I called Blimp to get on the meat. Blimp left the vegetable room and I was alone there with Kilrow. I hit Kilrow a punch and knocked him cold.

Then I ran out and passed the meat on the other side of the line. Cantofanti came out to me and whispered in my ear: "I poured a bucket of water on him and he didn't even move. He looks dead." I went over to the chef and said: "There's a guy lying on the floor in the back room."

We both went back there. He wouldn't come to. They got a stretcher and lugged him to the hospital and the doctor sent him to the Norfolk Prison Hospital immediately to get a spinal tap. He had a severe concussion and was paralyzed for two days. Then he got all right. The day he was punched, though, everybody was trying to find out who did it. But Blimp and the peep men held their mud and nobody found out. That very afternoon, the loudspeaker blared: "Barboza, report to Control." I said: "Fuck! They found out." When I got to Control, they said the warden wanted to see me. I went into his office and he said: "You're going outside the wall tomorrow to work."

The Blimp called me a "motherfucker."

I said: "Deputy Dawg, you got a mean punch."

I went outside the wall to work. It wasn't bad. I would go into the woods and meet people waiting for me. I'd put on a sports coat and drive off in a car with them for two hours at a time, eating in various restaurants. I'd go swimming. I was given cash, a hundred dollars at a time, to buy food through a screw I knew. We used to go fishing. We cooked out there. You name it and we did it. I even had rabbits out there that I bred.

In 1960 I went home on parole. I left my half of the bookmaking inside the prison to Joe Brazil, Jimmy "the Bear" Flemmi and Jimmy Parker. I left my half of the shylock business to Cantofanti. I went out to work at Scooterland and to fight professional.

2

It was my first job. Eddie Fisher owned Scooterland and my fight contract. That's how he swung my parole. Fisher was partners with Dave Winn, Gus Blaustein and Leo Swartz. Leo was a partner of Bernie McGarry who was real heavy in the numbers action and had connections with the politicians.

Scooterland was in the Motor Mart Building in back of the Hotel Statler. I worked there nine months and was made assistant manager. I talked Eddie into giving me money to shylock. In one year I turned $2,000 into $25,000, and it was on the street working to make more.

Sam Roseman came to work at Scooterland. He was an ex-convict. I had known his stepson at the Norfolk Prison Colony. Sam gave me a 1952 Dodge. He had just got another car. I was elated. I had never owned a car. Now, all I needed was a license. Leo Swartz sent me to the Corey brothers who were bondsmen. They spoke to an inspector who gave me a test and passed me. Now I had my license. The car would drive crazy and conk out. In time I found out it was due to the wrong type of voltage regulator, but one morning in front of my house the car wouldn't start. I jumped on my scooter and went looking for Tony Brazzo. Ran into Guy Frizzi. I had been introduced to him before but we just said hello and that was all. This time I explained my car wouldn't start. He went back with me and fiddled around and got it started. I went and had coffee with him. We got friendly and started going to the lounges at night.

Guy was, five feet, eight inches, with jet black hair and a dark complexion. He was a few years older than me and of Sicilian extraction. He walked around like George Raft and acted like him. He swore and used the filthiest language around girls and would think nothing about slapping one. He wore glasses and still had the plate for his two front teeth that he got in the Concord Reformatory in the late forties.

One night we walked into Alphonso's Clam House. Some blonde by the name of Sterling was singing there that night. She used to go with Tony Sasso, but he was missing and I knew he was dead. Skinny Spindale was the doorman. I knew Skinny. I had done time with his brother.

We sat down with Skinny and the blonde singer at a table near the corner of the stage. A red-headed guy with two shtarkers was sitting a few tables away. Alphonso came over and told us the red-headed guy was a big bookmaker from Malden. He was dangerous.

"Fuck him," said Guy Frizzi.

I was talking to the blonde about Sasso. Maybe I felt a little sorry for her. I think she knew what had happened. First thing I knew one of the men from the bookmaker's table came over and told Skinny not to throw his cigarette on the floor. Thought it might start a fire.

Skinny said: "That's my job. Go back and sit down."

I jumped up and said: "Look, we don't want no trouble. You want trouble, bother somebody else."

The man went back to his table and sat there, giving me the eye.

Guy said to the shtarker: "What are you looking at?"

He got up and came over and they started swinging at each other—Guy Frizzi and the fire marshal. I wanted to end it quick because I was still on parole so I stepped in and stuck him with a shank of a bottle. He didn't even know he was stabbed and kept fighting. Guy's glasses came off. He was blind without them.

"Fuck the parole," I said. I stepped in, hit him two punches and knocked him out. Then I looked at the big bookmaker who was still sitting there.

"Fuck you and Malden."

He didn't say nothing.

It was my first fight on account of Guy Frizzi. I didn't know when I met Guy it was like getting *il malocchio*, but before it was over I got the full curse—evil eye and all.

3

You might say Tony Sasso's troubles began right after I got out of Walpole. When I got out the first thing I had to do was get rid of $20,000 worth of jewelry with the price tags still on. It was a favor for a friend. He had done favors for me while he was out. Once when he couldn't buy any benny pills for me on the street, he stuck up a drugstore and got them. So when he got sent back just as I was getting out, he asked me to get this jewelry his wife had stashed. He needed the money to pay a lawyer so he could get back out. So I looked up Sasso. I had chummed around with him in prison.

First of all, let me explain about jewelry. When you see a $400 ring in the window, chances are that ring cost the retail dealer $200 at the Jewelers' Building in that city and cost the middleman $150 at the wholesale house in New York. The value you get on hot jewelry from a fence is one-third the wholesale value, or $50 for a $400 ring.

Sasso introduced me to Bobby Cardillo. We went to Revere with the jewelry and got $2,000 for it. I was a little disappointed, but Sasso said the rings were overpriced. So I gave the money to my friend's wife and she was satisfied.

I found out the truth later from "Gunner" Luciano who hung around with Sasso and was getting sick of the games Sasso played. He came to me at Scooterland and told me that Sasso and Cardillo got $2,600 for that jewelry and had held out on me.

It made me pretty mad especially since Sasso knew the money was for my friend who needed a lawyer.

Well, soon after that Sasso wasn't around no more. And I grabbed Cardillo and said: "You didn't know me well so you beat me. But I found out and someday I'll return the favor 'cause what goes around comes around."

Cardillo began to worry. Every time I saw him I just smiled at him.

In 1964 he was working for Henry Tameleo, handling truckloads of hot whiskey, hi-jacked cigarettes, stolen TV's, washing machines and clothing. He used to store them in garages and two warehouses he rented. When I got affiliated with Tameleo I still just smiled at Cardillo. Then one day I put some powdery stuff called "Scat" in his drink at the Ebbtide in Revere. Cardillo ran to the restroom puking with shit running down his legs. I let it be known that I did it. He just looked at me and then he started giving me things: TV's, rain-and-shine coats, cases of booze and cigarettes.

I got over $5,000 worth of stuff from him for that $600 he stole.

4

Gus Blaustein, who was one of the partners in Scooterland, gave me a job at Duffy's Lounge in Nantasket on the beach. It was a part-time job as bouncer on Friday, Saturday and Sunday nights. I had a few fights in Duffy's and outside and finally got the place quieted down so respectable people could sit down comfortably. I ended my first season there making a lot of friends. I don't know how it started but when I came back the second season I heard people were calling me "the King of the Jews." I didn't resent it. In fact I felt rather honored because I sure had some fine Jewish friends. We had some fine brawls together too.

One of them was outside in the amusement park which Gus and Davey Baker owned. There were about seven guys harassing the man who ran the gocart rides. They were from Randolph. I put myself near the two biggest guys. The fight just exploded out of thin air. I stepped to the side and let go with a left hook. One of the big boys went flying. Gus jumped on top of him and was looking like a champ. I pivoted to the other biggie and threw a right hand that went over his shoulder. He grabbed me in a bear hug. He was strong. I was pinned tight. With my hand around his head, I pulled his face to mine and clamped on with my teeth. With my other hand I pushed his chin away while holding on with my teeth. The meat on his cheek started to rip away. He screamed and let go. I spit out the flesh and blood and hit him three punches. He went down. The cops came and I went into the backway of Duffy's. I could taste the blood in my mouth all night no matter how many times I rinsed it out with Cokes.

Gus came to me the following weekend and warned me that the son of the police captain was around and was a troublemaker. Whatever you do, Gus said, don't have no run in with him. I promised.

The night wore on. About midnight a guy came to me and said this other guy was afraid to go out because a couple of punks were waiting for him outside. I went to investigate. Two guys were out there. One was a skinny runt about nineteen and the other was better than six feet and two hundred pounds. I said: "What is it, dude?"

The tall one said: "None of your fucking business."

I said: "Anything that happens on this sidewalk in front of this lounge is my business. Get out of here."

"Fuck you," said the tall one. He reached in his pocket. I thought he was going for a knife so I hit him a left hook that spun his head around and I threw a right hand that caught his jaw. Down he went. Later, when he got up, he fell down again, right on his face.

Gus, who had come out, grabbed my arm. "Leave it," he said. "It's the captain's son."

The next night Gus said to me: "The captain and his older son are parked outside. The son is a detective."

I looked out and saw the captain coming across the street. I spun around and went to the phone as he came in. He started hassling Rocco Balliro thinking he was me. I went out the back door and headed back to Boston. The captain told Gus he knew I was a pro fighter and on parole and he was going to send me back to prison on a parole violation for using dangerous weapons—my fists.

It was serious so I went to Leo Swartz who paid off a lot of politicians. Leo said: "Bernie McGarry had a crap game down there ten years ago. He knows people and he'll straighten it out."

Bernie and Leo had to go down there two nights in a row. The captain wanted $2,000 but finally accepted $1,000, which Gus and Davey had to pay. They didn't like it much and neither did I.

The captain had a lobster boat. Shortly after all this happened he was found out in the water all tangled up in his lobster pots. Drowned.

5

I was sitting in the corner booth at Duffy's Lounge when three classy foxes walked in. All sported wedding rings. They sat down at the bar facing me but I thought nothing of it. Later in the afternoon in comes this construction worker. He was married to a girl who ran a beauty parlor but they were on the outs and he was drunk and feisty. He came up to the booth and said to me: "If I want you I got you cold. Before you get untangled out of that booth your ass is mine."

My hand was on my knee under the table. In a second I grabbed the open knife I kept stuck in the bottom side of the table and had it waiting an inch under his protruding chin. He looked down at six inches of cold German steel and he blanched and shivered. Then he said: "I swear I'll never come up against you again."

Gus had come by in time to see the tail end of it. He was pleased since one of the foxes at the bar was the wife of the construction worker and Gus was making it with her. He went to tell her what had happened and the other two foxes listened in. I walked outside and crossed the street to a pavilion where bands used to play. Sitting on the railing, I enjoyed the view of the ocean and the smell of salt air. The fox found me there.

In natural light she was much prettier—truly a breathtaking girl. She said she had been looking at me for three weekends and I had never looked at her. "Everybody on the whole beach talks constantly about you," she said.

I blushed. She said her name was Cheryl. We spent an hour out there talking and finally Gus came out to see what had happened to me. I asked Cheryl if she'd like to wait for me till closing time and I would drive her home. She agreed. We ate and I drove her home but we got out and walked the beach at Hull until the sun came up. She was married to an attorney and was very secure and very unhappy. She looked like a miniature Sophia Loren with her swan-like features. I walked her home and then went home myself.

Next week she called the gym where I was training and asked if I'd be at Duffy's that weekend. "I want to give you something," she said.

She came in that weekend wearing a white on white slack outfit and with her hair flowing down her back raven black. She was five feet, three, and weighed one hundred and ten pounds and had sparkling blue eyes. We went to the pavilion and she handed me a little package. Inside was an expensive gold lighter. I said: "Can I kiss you?"

She said: "Yes, Joe, I want you to."

I held her in my arms and could feel the softness, the woman strength of her body and her full soft lips take mine and her open mouth and the expertness of her tongue. I don't know who felt the weakest from it—her or I. But I had to force myself away from her. She just stood there, her face all soft, and said: "I just knew it would be like that, Joe."

I said: "I wish it wasn't 'cause you got a husband." She said: "He hasn't been a husband in the four years I've been married to him."

The evening went by. She suggested I drive her straight home. I did. She told me the house was empty. Nobody was home or would be there that weekend. It was a beautiful expensive house on the beach. We entered the hallway and stepped into a sunken living room. It was just out of sight. She took me to her bedroom. It was carpeted in a soft black angora. A huge round bed covered with a gold spread was off to one side. Half the ceiling was mirrored and a gigantic, colorful butterfly was painted on the other half. There were speakers sunk into the wall and ceiling and when she put them on I heard Sarah Vaughn come piping through singing "Poor Butterfly." She turned another switch and the room became dimly lighted and a crystal ball turned causing different colors to sparkle off the walls and ceiling. It was some show.

Cheryl knew I smoked grass and she opened a drawer and offered me one of about twenty joints she had there. I said: "Can I kiss you again?"

She just came into my arms. Then we took off our clothes and she went into the bathroom. I lay on the bed and smoked. She came out naked, built like a living goddess, her breasts upturned and no slack on her anywhere. She sat down on the foot of the bed and started to suck on my big toe. I freaked out at first, never having had this happen to me, but the pressure from her mouth caused me slowly to get an erection. Slowly she came up on each side of my legs and thighs with nips, licks and kisses, until she had her tongue darting in and out of my anus. At first I felt defiled with the act of it, but then I started digging it. She came back and made love to the erection I had, and it was like nobody had ever done before. She kept saying I had the biggest one she ever saw.

All through the night we made love to the music of "Born Free" on the stereo.

The weeks went by and our love affair continued. Then I

broke the jaw of the police captain's son and I was sweating. Suddenly I wanted out of Nantasket and away from this girl. I came up with an idea to fake her out. I told her I had to have $3,000 or I'd have to go away. She asked if I'd be in Nantasket next day and I said I would. Next day she said: "I have $3,000 for you."

I looked at her and I felt like a punk. How could I do this to someone who loved me? So I told Cheryl I didn't need the money after all.

But the affair soon ended. I kept picking fights with her over her husband and the fact that I couldn't give her the things he had given her. We soon broke up but stayed friends. Years later when I testified against Jerry Anguilo, she was in the courtroom and blew me a kiss. I knew we'd always have fond memories of each other until the day we died. It sounds corny, but that's the way it was.

6

Things were going pretty good. I was shylocking on my own out of North Station and I was fighting strong too. *Ring Magazine* made me the light-heavyweight fighter of the month for September, and I had dreams of going all the way.

I was living in East Boston and hitting the nightspots regularly. One night Guy and Connie Frizzi and two other guys came by and we went into town and made the rounds. We ended up at the Peppermint Lounge. It was 1:30 A.M. when the joint closed. We went walking out together with Connie and Guy leading the way. As I got to the entrance I heard Connie say: "Hi, Bush."

The girl he spoke to was pretty but she wasn't alone. With her was another girl and two big men. One of the men was wearing a black cashmere topcoat. He turned around to Connie and said: "What did you say?"

Connie and the man started swinging. Guy jumped

in. The man saw Connie's and Guy's faces but he didn't see the faces of the other two men in our party. They were so bunched up on the sidewalk which was loaded with people that they couldn't get any room. I figured I wasn't needed to add to the confusion so I stood at the curb watching it. The man in the cashmere coat suddenly went down, stabbed by one of our men. We all started running down the street and somebody started firing a gun at us.

Connie yelled: "The guy had a gun."

We ran around the corner on Broadway into Sal Casario's store and hid.

Next day the papers were screaming: "Joe Parillo, police officer, war hero, has his coat pulled over his head and is stabbed while investigating loansharks. His wife waits bravely at his side."

There was a picture of the wife. I said: "That isn't the girl he was with at the Peppermint Lounge."

A lot of people had recognized me and they told the police. The police picked me up at my home and made a big show by blocking off the street. There was a lot of heat and they wanted the public to think they were doing their job. I was the patsy.

They questioned me all night at Station Four. Because I was an up and coming fighter, the officers at the station treated me all right. Station Four is a place where they think nothing of breaking your skull. I caught the crabs from staying there all night. Then they took me before the police officer who got stabbed. We went over to City Hospital to see him. He said to me: "Did you see me in the Peppermint Lounge?"

I said: "Yes, sir, but it wasn't with the girl standing outside the door." The cop's eyes opened wide. He said: "This isn't one of the men. He is too big."

I said: "Thank you" and went home to get rid of the crabs.

7

It was January 1, 1962. Leo Swartz called me at home. "I'm at Duffy's place in Chelsea. Get over here right away."

It sounded serious so I called Tony Brazzo and told him to bring a gun and come along. Then I went down into the cellar, checked the Luger I carried, put two shells into a sawed-off shotgun and strapped it on my shoulder. Then I covered it all up with a rain-and-shine coat and went to meet Tony. We drove over to the Harmony Lounge in Chelsea. I told Tony to keep the motor running and I went into the lounge with my hand stuck through the slash pocket holding the shotgun. My coat was open so I would have no trouble reaching in with my other hand and grabbing the front of the shotgun to swing it out into firing position. But just inside the lounge I saw a cop, so I wheeled around and went back to the car and took the shotgun off my shoulder. Then I went back clean with Tony coming along.

Leo spotted me and came over. Leo said: "They just stuck up the place this morning for $60,000. This lounge is the main office for all the bookmaking action in Chelsea, part of Everett, Revere and East Boston. The pickup men leave all the money here."

I said: "What do you want me for?"

Leo said: "I want you to meet some people and then I want to ask you about a guy I think fits the description of who did this."

We went over to a booth. Leo said: "I want you to meet Joe Burns."

Joe Burns was a man in his fifties, probably handsome once. He was six feet and chubby. I was later to learn his real name was Joseph Anselmo and he was head man for the Mafia in Chelsea.

Leo said: "I want you to meet Hymie Abrams."

Hymie was also in his fifties. He had a medium build and a ruddy face. He was back from Vegas for the holidays and a medical checkup. Hymie made his money in the bootlegging days and now he fronted for the Office of the Sands Hotel in Las Vegas.

Leo said: "I want you to meet Ralphie Chong."

Chong was in his middle forties. His real name was Ralph Lamattina. People called him Chong because his father used to have dealings in Chinatown. Ralphie was only five feet, six, and his waist was wider than his shoulders. At this time he was an enforcer for Anselmo. People talked about him chasing Jackie Lupo down the streets of the North End and stabbing him five times.

Leo said to all of them: "Joe is with me."

Anselmo said: "If those guys get picked up by the cops, I don't want nobody to identify them in the lineup. We'll handle it ourselves. I want to make an example out of them." Leo said to me: "Joe, one of the guys was a redhead with a high pitched voice. He seemed nervous and was of medium height and build. Does that fit Red Mericki?"

I thought for a minute. Red Mericki was a friend of mine and I wasn't going to finger him or nobody else. I said: "No, I don't think so. I was with him in the old Charlestown prison and I worked with him outside the wall at Walpole. Red is soft-spoken and chunky. He hasn't got a nervous bone in his body. A score like this wouldn't faze him."

They took my word for it. Leo gave me a plug to Ralphie Chong. Ralphie said: "Joe, you come over to the North End and see me. Don't be a stranger. I've heard a lot of good things about you and I'm glad to meet you and to know you're with Leo."

We shook hands. Even his hands were puny.

I went over to the North Station next day and saw Vinnie "the Pig" DiVincent who traveled with Red Mericki. I told the Pig the story and told him to tell Red.

Later on they found out who the red-headed robber was. It was Jack O'Banowitz, an ex-con, but by the time they found out, Jack was a convict again in New Hampshire. And for a long time too.

8

I walked into the Surf Club down at Revere Beach. The Surf was the Frolics' biggest competition and it was owned by Peter DeCarlo, a friend of mine. Guy Frizzi was with me. The joint was packed. I bumped into a girl.

"Excuse me," I said. "I'm terribly sorry."

Her boyfriend said: "On your way, faggot."

I recognized him. I had seen him in the North End on School Street behind a pushcart.

I was shocked. I said: "What did you say?" Then some guy reached over Pushcart's shoulder and punched me in the chin.

I was shocked again. I didn't even feel the punch.

The guy who threw it started yelling: "Ralphie Chong is my brother-in-law and Henry Tag is my brother."

I said: "Don't be loud-talking Ralphie's name." To Pushcart I said: "Punk, I'll see you later." Then I ran out of the Surf. Guy, who hadn't said a word, followed me out.

We stood in the parking lot. Guy asked: "What are you going to do?"

I said: "I don't know, but I'm going to fuck them up.

Peter DeCarlo came out. Peter said: "Joe, I'm sure sorry that happened in there."

I said: "Peter, I ran out of your place because I didn't want to upset your crowd."

He said: "Thanks, Joe. Come back in."

I said: "No, Peter."

Peter went back inside. Ten minutes later Ralphie Chong's brother-in-law came out. His name was Joe Tag, I found out later. As soon as he came out, Peter turned off the parking lot lights. It was nice and dark.

Joe Tag, five foot, seven, of medium build, came out with his topcoat thrown open and his hands deep in his pockets and a stub of a cigar sticking out of his mouth. He said: "I've put one guy in a hole already."

I said: "Is your hole the only one in the woods?"

Then I hit him with an arched left hook. He slammed to the ground out cold. Guy and I left in our car with Guy laughing like hell.

They carried Joe Tag inside the club for all to see. He was moaning and groaning and they put cold towels on his face. His jaw was fractured.

I called Leo Swartz and told him what happened. Then I said: "The reason I'm telling you is because I don't want Ralphie Chong to ask what kind of a piece of shit you introduced him to. Meaning me."

Next day Leo called and put Ralphie on. Ralphie said: "I talked to my other brother-in-law who was there and he said you were right and Tag did scream my name out. You should have stabbed the punk."

I said: "I wish it didn't happen, Ralph."

"Never mind," said Ralph. "Did you really hit him just one punch?"

I said: "Yes."

Ralphie hung up. He went to see Joe Tag and slapped him in the jaw which was all wired up.

"That's for mentioning my name," Ralphie said.

I went over to School Street and grabbed the Pushcart.

"This is your friendly fag," I said. I just slapped him around and kicked him. Guy gave him a kick too. We left him balled up on the ground screaming, "I'm sorry."

9

I was in Leo Swartz's dry-cleaning shop on Massachusetts Avenue. If you looked at the setup carefully you would have noticed something amiss. Behind the counter was a clothes rack. The clothes hanging on it with tags on them looked like clothing from the Roaring Twenties. They were dusty too. Two men leaned on the counter reading the sports section and two others were playing cards behind the partition.

I said: "Where is Leo?"

"In back," said Billy the peep man.

I went around the clothes rack and through the partition into the back room. Tables with chairs and benches were scattered about and there was a blackboard on the wall with the race results and the payoffs. I went through the crowd and opened the half door with the counter on it that served as a betting window. Behind the rail was a table with an intercom. Leo was sitting there, reading bets to a man on the second floor.

"Hi, Leo," I said.

Leo said: "I'll be with you in a second."

When he got all the bets in, he said: "I want to talk to you. Let's go down to the cellar."

We went down to the cellar. Leo said: "I was talking to Peter Limone. Peter wants a bundle job done on a guy. I mentioned your name, Joe, and Peter said you'd be fine."

I said: "What's the scam?"

Leo said: "It involves this guy who is running for the presidency of the Baker's Union at the baking factory near North Station."

We discussed it. I got all the dope on where the dude lived in Dorchester, plate number of his car and the car's make and color, the guy's description, and where he parked in the parking lot by the factory. I left Leo's place feeling pretty good on this day in 1962 because I was slowly climbing the ladder. This job would put me in solid where the real money was.

Things were going well. I was still shylocking and still fighting. Scooterland had closed but I had a front job at an auto agency Eddie Fisher owned, and I was in love with a blonde who worked there.

I went to see a couple of friends named Tony and Joe and they agreed to help me although I told them there wouldn't be any money in it since I wanted to show some class and do it for nothing. They understood that it might lead to bigger things if we handled it right.

A couple of weeks went by and I was ready. To top it off, a hurricane was in the making. All the people were closing shop getting ready for it, and there was rain and it was already dark. Tony and Joe got another ex-con named Phil to help out. He was a right-on dude and we decided he would drive the hot car we had picked up for the job.

We drove by the parking lot and saw the baker in his car leaving the lot early. We sped away to his house, getting there ahead of him. It was beautifully stormy. Nobody was on the street.

His car came by the hot car where three men waited. The car immediately pulled out and when the dude opened his door and got out on the sidewalk two men were there. One hit him in the head with a sash weight made of cast iron. The dude ran out into the middle of the street. The two men pursued him, beating him with sash weights. They left the baker a bloody heap in the street and jumped into the hot car. Phil gunned the motor and the car went to where Tony's car was waiting. Then we drove to Leo's place. I told the others to wait and I went downstairs with Leo.

I said: "It's all done."

Leo said: "How did it go?"

I said: "You'll read about it in the papers."

Leo pulled out a roll of bills. "Here is a thousand."

I said: "I don't want it. You've done a lot for me and I've never done nothing for you."

Leo said: "All right. Let me pay expenses."

"The expenses were one dollar for two sash weights," I said. "I'll see you later."

The papers had the story—and pictures. The victim had a broken shoulder, busted ribs, sixteen stitches on his leg, and a cut on his forehead. Leo was pleased and Peter Limone thanked me.

2

The Lure of Danger

In September, 1962, Joe Barboza was adjudged guilty of parole violation and was returned to prison to finish the sentence imposed in 1958. The blonde he had met at the auto agency promised to wait for him if, in the interval, he converted to Judaism. He agreed. On April 30, 1964, he was released. It marked the first time since 1945 that he had been free of state supervision. Ironically, this chance to make a new beginning came at the very moment the simmering McLean—McLaughlin feud broke into open warfare. This despite an FBI report of March 29, 1963, that Georgie McLaughlin had risen in the world and appeared "to be working as an aide or assistant in the Office of Governor Endicott Peabody." Barboza determined to stay out of the war, but tales of headless bodies have a certain fascination for an action man.

1

On the day I got out of Walpole I married my blonde girlfriend up in Maine. Then we headed for Rhode Island for a honeymoon. We stopped off at Guy Frizzi's house in East Boston. They had a cake for us. I was introduced to Chico Amico and his wife, Janet. Guy and I were going to be partners and Guy said he'd like to have Chico work for us. I told him we'd talk about it later since I had other things on my mind that day.

My wife and I went on to the Colonial Motor Inn along the bay in Rhode Island. We had a suite at the inn. On May 2, 1964, three days after I got out of prison, Guy called. "Did you hear the news?" Guy asked. "They found a body in the trunk of a car with his head missing."

"His head missing!" I said. "Did they identify the body?"

"No," Guy said. "Hey, Joe, when are you going to start back for home?"

"I guess I'll start back Sunday about noon."

"That's good," Guy said. "You got to chase down a lot of money that was hanging in the air while you were in the can."

"Yeah," I said. "I've got about ten thousand loose out there on the street that's been dead these last twenty months."

Sunday evening I met Guy in East Boston. "Did they find out who that stiff in the trunk of the car was yet?" I asked.

"Yeah," Guy said. "It was some ex-con by the name of Francis Benjamin."

"Frank Benjamin," I said. "That dude just got out a couple of weeks ago. I've known him since he was a kid. He was a tough southpaw and a right-on mother."

A few days later Guy and I were inside the Baker's Dozen Coffee Shop on the corner of Bennington and Brooks. It was about two in the afternoon. I said: "Well, I've got back eighty-five hundred and it's working for me already. Not bad, huh Dirty Feet."

"That's real good, Joe," Guy said. "You shook up North Station with some of the beatings you gave. They won't forget to come up with it regular now."

The door to the doughnut shop swung open and in walked Blu Di'Agostino. I said: "Hey, Blu, good to see you."

Blu said: "Joe, I heard you were home. Good to see you. Guy turned his back. He didn't like Di'Agostino. Blu said: "You hear about that guy, Benjamin?"

I said: "Yeah, man, I knew him well."

Blu lowered his voice. "I heard a guy by the name of Jimmy did it. They call him 'the Bear.' Know him?"

I said: "Not really."

We talked awhile and eventually Blu left. I turned to Guy and said: "After dinner tonight we're going to see a friend of mine."

"Who is he?"

I said: "The Bear—Jimmy Flemmi."

"But you told Blu you really didn't know him."

I said: "Do you think I'd tell that big mouth anything? Who the hell is he to mention the Bear's name in something like the Benjamin case?"

About 8 P.M., Guy and I drove through the Summer Tunnel heading for Dearborn Square, Roxbury. We were in Guy's gold 1962 Caddie convertible. We spotted the Bear in the doorway of a restaurant across the street from a bar where I used to meet Leo Swartz. The bar had burned down since then.

"Hey Jimmy," I yelled.

Jimmy came over and got in the car. "Gotta watch it," he said. "The area is loaded with law."

I said: "Fine thing. I just got out and I got to come to see you. You're too good to come and see me, huh?"

The Bear said: "Man, I've got more heat on me! I did you a favor by not coming by now."

I introduced Guy Frizzi as my partner. They shook hands and said hello. Then I told the Bear about Blu and his big mouth.

"I don't know no Di'Agostino," said the Bear. "He must have heard the law picked me up and questioned me about it. The law said they think you did it."

"Me?" I said. "Motherfucker, use that psych on somebody else."

The Bear laughed and said: "Here's what happened."

A couple of weeks before the bar across the street burned down, Benjamin, Wimpy Bennett and some people were in it. Benjamin was loaded and was blubbering about how he was on the McLean side and how he was going to whack out all the McLaughlin crowd he could. Wimpy got to a phone and called Punchie McLaughlin. Punchie said he'd be down in an hour and to keep Benjamin there.

Benjamin tried to leave and Wimpy shot him at the bar and dragged him into a storage room. An hour went by and Punchie still hadn't come. Wimpy went in back to check Benjamin who was crawling around. Blood was everywhere. Wimpy was shocked. He thought the dude was dead and here he was crawling around. Wimpy shot him again in the head. A little while later Punchie showed up.

"Where is he?" Punchie asked.

Wimpy said: "He's in the back room dead."

Punchie asked: "How many people seen you do it?"

"About fifteen," said Wimpy.

"The law is going to check this place out for blood because fifteen people aren't going to hold their mud," Punchie said.

Wimpy said: "After we move him out I'll soak the place down and torch it."

"Okay," Punchie said, "but first I want to work on him."

Wimpy said: "Whatta you mean?" Punchie said:

"I want to saw his head off and leave it on Ballou's doorstep so he can think about it." Ballou was a friend of Benjamin and on the McLean side.

Wimpy said: "Do what you want." Punchie got a saw and they went in the back room and Punchie sawed off Benjamin's head. He was wrapping it in a plastic bag when he saw the bullet holes.

"Look at them holes," said Punchie. "Is the gun clean?"

Wimpy said: "Son of a bitch! I got the gun off a cop and I don't know if it's clean or not."

Punchie said: "Well, that means the head can't be found at all. We'll leave Benjamin in the trunk of a car and bury the head in the woods."

"Good," Wimpy said. "We'll put him in a car I keep ready and then we'll burn the place and go bury the head."

They put Benjamin's body in the trunk of a car and put the head on the floor in the back of the car. Then they went inside the bar and soaked it from top to bottom in gasoline, lit a match and the lounge went up like a match box. They drove off in two cars—Wimpy in his own car and Punchie driving the one with the cut-up in it. They left the car with the torso somewhere and Punchie got in with Wimpy and drove off with the head.

When they got to a wooded area and stopped, Punchie said: "Give me the gun."

Wimpy said: "What for?"

Punchie said: "Well, I'm not going into the woods with no gun while you got one."

Wimpy said: "Well, if that's the way you feel then I'm not giving up my gun. Your attitude is giving me bad vibrations."

They looked at each other.

Wimpy said: "I'll drive you to your car."

He did. Then Punchie said: "Where are you going now?"

Wimpy said: "I'm taking my head and leaving."

"That's the story," said the Bear.

Guy sat there dumbfounded. I said: "I don't know which is colder: sawing off the head or those paranoid cuckoos in the woods. Sure is a cold story."

"See you tomorrow," said the Bear.

2

When I got married I converted to Judaism for the sake of my wife and I had my name legally changed to Baron. I was circumcised at Beth Israel and while I was still stitched up I didn't want to use a filthy bathroom.

One day I went into Benbrook Drugstore on the corner of Bennington and Brooks Street. I'd been in there before and I'd always been polite and soft-spoken in contrast to my partner, Guy Frizzi, who got respect by insulting people.

I said: "Al, can I use your bathroom?"

"No," he said, "because I use it."

I said: "If I was a hooker, it'd be all right. If Guy asked you, it'd be all right. But because I don't fuck over you and demand respect, you take that for weakness and mouth off to me. Well, I'm not threatening you; I'm promising you."

That night Nicky, Chico and I broke all the windows in his store at midnight. When we got there next morning the windows were all plywood. The Bear asked what happened. I told him. The Bear said: "Go ask him if you can use his bathroom now."

So I did. I walked in and said: "Can I use your bathroom?"

Al said: "Sure, go ahead, Joe." I went ahead.

Chico was working for us at a hundred a week. Nicky Fernia only got seventy-five, but that was because twenty-five went to pay interest on a $600 loan we bought up from Yogi Brazzo because Nicky didn't like Yogi's big mouth. Nicky never did get around to paying off that loan.

One night we were at Chico's home. Chico's wife wasn't there. Chico, Nicky and I were smoking grass in the kitchen. Guy came in with Ellie, his girlfriend. She was five feet, eight inches, and size forty-two breasts. Silicone. She had a hard face and was a little stir-crazy.

Guy winked at me. Then he said: "You guys are all jealous over my broad. Well, fuck you, she's mine. Aren't you, honey?"

Ellie, in her peabrain voice, said: "Yes, Guy."

Then Guy said: "They all want to feel your beautiful tits, but they can't. Only me. Right, honey?"

"Right," said Ellie.

Guy grabbed her breasts and said to us: "Drool! They're mine and you guys can't touch."

Guy was winking at us all the time.

He lifted her dress and said: "Did you ever see legs like that?"

Ellie smirked and Guy said: "Do you love me, Ellie?"

"Yes, Guy."

"Then let's make them real jealous." He unzipped his pants and helped Ellie take her clothes off. Ellie got down on her knees and grabbed a mouthful. All the while Guy was saying: "Make them drool."

Then the thing that blew my mind happened. Guy said: "Let me put it in your ear."

Sure enough. The dizzy broad sticks it in her ear and is going back and forth with her head. We all laughed until tears came out of our eyes but I could never stomach that peabrained broad again.

3

Tony Brazzo, ex-con, shylock, thief, enforcer and a friend of mine, was in love. The girl was married and the husband, a meek little man, used to beg Tony to stay away from her. Tony tried to make the husband understand the girl didn't love him—the husband—anymore, but the guy just wouldn't give up.

Actually, Tony was a pretty big operator with connections to the Office through the Gold Dust Twins, Joe Russo and Vinnie DeCissio. So when the husband shot Tony in the back of his head late one night, I went to the wake with Guy Frizzi. I'd been out of Walpole a little over two months, and I was wearing a gray silk mohair suit. The wake was in the funeral parlor in Maverick Square. I was standing near the rear door when it opened and in came Joe Russo and Peter Limone with another man. Russo said: "Henry, I want you to meet Joe Barboza. Joe, this is Henry Tameleo."

We shook hands and that was the first time I met Tameleo who ran the Office in Boston for Raymond Patriarca, the Mafia boss of all New England. Limone was high up in the organization, but Henry was near the top. He hung out down at the Ebbtide which had just opened in Revere.

Well, we talked awhile and I was glad to know him, but that was about it until some weeks later when Chico told me about Ninni Frizzi getting beat up at the Ebbtide. Now Ninni was Guy and Connie Frizzi's younger brother, and that made it my business. Chico said Arthur and Junior Ventola ganged up on Ninni when he complained about a watered drink.

When Guy and Connie heard the news we headed for the Ebbtide—five of us in one car. I had a baseball bat in my lap. Only the cleanup men were at the Ebbtide when we got there at 9:30 A.M. so we went on to Arthur Ventola's vegetable store on the Revere highway. It was called "Arthur's Farm." When we got there we found Arthur and a retarded guy he kept around to run errands. I ran over to Arthur, who was an ex-con in his early fifties and big, swinging my bat and yelling, "You motherfucking punk."

I swung at his head and he got his hands in front of his face just as the bat crashed across them. He bent over and I swung the bat twice off his back and once off the back of his head. That sent him crashing to the floor. He started blubbering: "It was Junior, my brother, that hit Ninni."

We started off to find Junior. Just as we were getting in the car, Louis Grieco pulled up. Connie Frizzi and Louis were partners so he joined us. We didn't find Junior. Later we learned that he had holed up in a girl's pad for three weeks and then slithered off to Florida. While he was hiding, the

Mafia wheels began turning. Ronnie Casesso called me and said: "Joe, Henry Tameleo would like it very much if you would do him a favor and forget the rest of the Ventola beef."

I said: "Ronnie, I've no say in this matter. Guy is my partner. I'm along in a show of strength. All I know is those two pieces of shit, Arthur and Junior, give twenty percent to the Office so they have the strength to run the Ebbtide. Those two had to buy strength and they let it go to their heads and thought they could hit a man's brother who is connected with the Office. Connie Frizzi is connected with the Office because he has strength. Let the Frizzis give the answer. Like I said, I'm just muscle."

Ronnie said: "Joe, I understand. Henry would like you to drop by the Ebbtide any chance you get. He promises you won't be insulted like that again."

While I was talking, Connie Frizzi was meeting with Henry. He agreed to forget the beef. When I heard about it, I said to Guy: "Look, if Connie plays politics at Ninni's expense, why the hell should I pursue it? At the least it should be settled by breaking that asshole Junior's legs. But I got nothing to say."

I went to the Ebbtide to see Henry Tameleo and it was the start of a friendship. I learned to admire and look up to Henry more than any man living. When we shook hands, Henry said: "Joe, this is what happens when you get involved with weak assholes. It gives them speech and they run off at the mouth because of your strength. I promise you'll never be insulted again like that in this joint."

I went back the next night and the next. Henry and I got along fine all the time Junior was gone. One weekend I walked in and Henry wasn't there. Arthur Ventola was sitting at a table. He smiled at me and gave me a big wave. Junior was standing there a little loaded. He turned around and saw me.

"What is he doing here?" Junior said. "I want him out."

I said: "Listen, Junior, you piece of shit. Henry said I wouldn't ever be insulted again in here."

He said: "I don't care; I want you out."

I said: "Let's go into the kitchen, you motherfucker."

He put his hand in his pocket and said: "Okay." I walked through the swinging doors and spun around just as he was in the middle of the doors. I grabbed him by his coat front, tugged him to me, and with my other hand I stuck a .38 automatic into his neck right under his chin.

"Now pull your right hand out of your pocket and do it nice and easy," I said, "or I'll blow your tonsils out the top of your head."

His hand came out with a paper-wrapped roll of dimes. I said: "You really believe you're a tough guy, you sick motherfucker?"

Richie Castucci, the nephew of the Ventolas and the brains in the family, came in the kitchen and said: "Joe, don't."

I turned to Richie and said:, "Henry promised I wouldn't be insulted in here, but I have been insulted so nobody must give a fuck. I'll straighten it out myself."

"It'll be straightened out," said Richie.

It was. Henry blew his top with Junior and bought him out. Now Henry and the Office owned forty percent. Castucci owned twenty percent, his aunt had twenty and Arthur had twenty.

A few months went by. I helped Henry keep the place quiet. The Office bought out Richie's aunt and Arthur, leaving only Richie who thought he was real tough with the Office's strength behind him.

It was funny, Ronnie Casesso would sit at one table and talk on the telephone to Richie's wife at another table. Richie would be strutting up and down in between while Ronnie told her how much he loved her and how he couldn't wait to get into her pants that night. All the time he talked, he kept looking at Richie and laughing.

4

I met Ronnie and Joe Dermandy at the Concord Reformatory when I was 17 years old. Both brothers were boxers and weight lifters. Upon release, Ronnie started seeing Red O'Toole's girl, Dottie, and eventually he fell in love with her. He thought about killing O'Toole himself, but he decided that wouldn't be proper so he went to Georgie McLaughlin with a proposition. If Georgie would kill O'Toole, leaving him free to marry Dottie, he would kill Buddy McLean for Georgie. In fact, to show good faith, he would kill McLean first.

He tried. One night on a dark street he took a shot at a dude he thought was Buddy McLean, but he missed. He then called up another guy named Buddy who had been with us at Concord. This Buddy, unknown to Dermandy, was very close to Buddy McLean.

On the phone, Dermandy said: "Hi, Buddy, I just took a shot at Buddy McLean."

The Buddy on the other end of the line froze for a second and then said: "Did you hit him?"

Dermandy said: "I think so, but I don't know if I killed him. Listen, I want to see you."

They made a date to meet two days later. Little Buddy, as the boys called him, hung up. Then he drove over to Winter Hill and walked into the Tap Royal and there stood Buddy McLean.

"Wow! Am I glad to see you," said Little Buddy. He told Buddy McLean the story. McLean said: "So you're going to meet him day after tomorrow?"

Little Buddy said: "Yep, and I'll handle it myself."

McLean said: "You want a car there with some backup men?"

"Nope," said Little Buddy. "I'll handle it myself."

And he did.

There were a lot of newspaper headlines, and editorials citing the murder of Ronnie Dermandy, ex-con, as additional proof that law and order had collapsed. Actually, the two Buddys acted quite civilized.

Buddy McLean said: "You've done enough, Buddy. I don't want nothing happening to you. Why don't you leave the state?"

Little Buddy decided it was a good idea. He went to California. About nine months later I was in the Tap Royal and Little Buddy called. Buddy McLean told me to say "Hi" to him, and Little Buddy told me he was having a ball out west.

Meanwhile, Joe Dermandy went crazy down at the Norfolk Prison Colony when he heard Ronnie had been killed. He swore to avenge him and even accused me of doing it. I sent him a message: "I can understand your grief but I didn't do it so don't blame me. Don't send me no more threats. I'll be here on the streets waiting for you."

Joe sent back word that he was sorry and he'd "straighten" it out when he got out.

Well, Joe Dermandy never got out. He was found stabbed to death in his room. He died in prison like his dad before him.

And the gang war went on.

5

One day in the summer of 1964, Guy Frizzi and I went back to Nantasket to see Gus Blaustein and other friends. We met my successor as bouncer there, a dude named Charlton Eaton. He asked Guy if Guy could get him a connection to push football bet cards. So later we took Eaton to Peter Limone at the Dog House in the North End and arranged for him to start pushing cards in the Nantasket and Quincy areas.

Some time later Limone told me that Eaton was beating

him on the cards and he had the proof. Limone said he'd have to have the cheater straightened out.

Around September 25, 1964, Eaton was down to our corner where Guy and I had our shylocking headquarters. The business was skyrocketing and we didn't want no trouble since we were taking two thousand a week out of it. I left Guy and Eaton about 4 P.M. and went home. That night, Eaton was found on Mingo Road in Malden. He was in the front seat of his late-model Caddie with two .38 caliber bullets in his head.

We got word from an attorney that for some reason the law was going to pick us up and question us about it. We took off to a place in New Hampshire. After we had been there awhile, I got bored and called Eddie Fisher, my old fight manager, to pick me up. He took me back to Boston and left me at his girl's pad in Kenmore Square. Her name was Shirley.

I remembered Shirley from the time I got out of Walpole in April. A little while after I got out some of the guys took me to a stag party. They had three young hookers from Rhode Island and another naked broad in her thirties who danced around and kept jumping into guys' laps and wiggling her ass. When she came to me, I said: "Don't do that," and stood up. She said: "Who do you think you are?" Eddie Fisher said: "What's the matter, Joe?" I said: "I've just had a girl wait twenty months for me to get out of prison, and I don't want no broad rubbing her asshole on my pants." Well, they understood. Shirley was one of the other hookers, and after the party Eddie started keeping her.

I stayed with Shirley until I could make some phone calls and then Guy, my attorney and I walked into the Malden Police Station and I was questioned. They didn't have anything solid, of course, so afterwards one of the cops said: "A lot of the fellows in the station wonder who would win if you and Buddy McLean had a fight."

I said: "Who is Buddy McLean?"

The cop laughed and said: "Get the hell out of here."

I got all the way to Las Vegas. I stayed at the Sands for ten days as a guest of Hymie Abrams, the old bootlegger. I rode Arabian horses in the desert, ate the most delicious food I've ever eaten, and visited Hoover Dam. With me was a female friend, and we lay around the pool a lot and saw all the fantastic nightclub acts Vegas is famous for. We even walked away from the crap tables some one hundred dollars ahead.

It was a memorable trip and I was very happy. The money was rolling in and, above all, I was going to be a father in seven months. I was sure the baby would never want for anything like I had.

We headed back for Boston and then tension all came back; the alertness for suckers, cops and hit men. The Eaton murder never was solved.

6

While sitting in the car with Chico and the Bear at Dearborn Square in Roxbury, I said: "This city is red hot over what happened to Iggy Lowery."

"Yeah," said the Bear. "They've been floating by here all day in their unmarked cars."

I said: "Iggy was a queer in the Old Charlestown prison when I was there."

The Bear said: "I found out what happened to him. Want to hear it?"

I said: "Does a bear shit in the woods?"

"Of course I do," said the Bear. "It all started when this dude walked into a bar and saw his brother's wife sitting with Iggy all cuddly. So this dude motioned to Iggy to come over because he didn't want the girl to hear. Then the dude said: "Say, man, that's my brother's wife. What the hell is it with you, Iggy?"

Iggy said: "Listen, *your* brother was trying to make *my* wife last night. Now it's my turn."

They passed a few more words and the dude left. A few hours later the bar closed and Iggy and the girl came out. The dude was waiting in a parked car. He called Iggy over again and told him to get in. Soon as he did the dude stepped on the gas and raced off, leaving the girl standing on the sidewalk.

Iggy yelled: "Let me out, you motherfucker."

The dude stopped the car, pulled out a four-shot derringer and shot Iggy in the head. It sure messed up the interior of the car. Then the dude took out a knife and started cutting Iggy's throat. He tried to cut the head off but the knife was too small. It messed up the car some more.

Finally, the dude gave up. He drove the car over to the corner where his brother hung out. The dude's brother was there. The dude called him over and said: "Look what I got."

The dude's brother looked and then jumped back. He said: "You crazy bastard! Why did you do it?"

The dude said: "Because he was a smartass, that's why. Now follow me in your car."

They drove to Pembrook and left Iggy in the car there. Then the dude went home with his brother.

"That's the story," said the Bear.

"Did the dude tell his brother why he killed Iggy?" I asked.

"No," said the Bear. "What was the point?"

A couple of weeks passed and the Bear came to my corner in East Boston. He said: "Read about the dude getting shot in the leg?"

"Yeah," I said. "Who did it?"

"The girl, his brother's wife. She was mad as hell at him for killing Iggy."

"Does the brother know she done it?" I asked.

"No," said the Bear. "What's the point?"

7

The shylock business can get complicated.

This guy that ran an auto insurance agency wanted me to collect some bad debts. I asked for some names. He said: "I let Sal Cesario borrow over a thousand." I said, "Forget it." He said: "I let Ralphie Chong borrow over a thousand." I said: "You got burnt." He tried again: "Joe Tebargio." I said: "I'll find out about that one."

I went to Arthur's Farm to see Johnny Revere who booked out of there for Red Assid. He called Red and made a date for me to see him at the club on Tyler Street. When I walked in I saw Tebargio in the corner, but I walked over to Red and told him: "I want to find out if Tebargio is with you and Biaoni. If he is, I'll forget it. If he ain't, I'll win some bread."

Red said: "He's with us, but come with me. I want him to hear this."

Tebargio looked like a sick Peter Lorre with a lot of hair. We went into the bathroom and Red told me to tell him about the debt. I did, and when I was through, Teabags—that's what Red called him—stepped toward me and pointed his finger.

"Listen to me," he began.

Red reached around me and slapped him. "You little big-mouthed asshole, this guy will kill you. He's a friend of ours and you'll respect him or I'll kick your teeth in."

I left and a few days later Johnny Revere, Red's bookie, came down to my corner and wanted to borrow $500. I told him to get it from Red. He said he didn't want Red to know. So I warned him: "Look, if you take my money, I don't care who you work for or how tough you are—you'll get stabbed if you don't pay."

Johnny said: "I'll pay, Joe."

I gave him $500 and said: "You owe me twenty-five dollars a week."

Four or five weeks went by and he paid. Then he didn't show up for four straight weeks and when he did he said he didn't have it. I said: "I told you you can get hurt, didn't I? You come up with all you're behind next week, do you hear?"

Johnny said: "Yes, Joe." I didn't see him again for nine weeks. I left notes on his car up in Orient Heights, East Boston. Still no Johnny. Then I spotted him driving his white convertible on Bennington Street. I followed him and stopped him on a corner near Pinky's place. I parked just in front of him and told Chico and Nicky to stay in the car. While I walked back to him I thought of all the aggravation he had caused me because he thought Red would protect him. Seeing me ask Red about collecting from Tebargio had given him the idea.

He pulled away as I looked in through the window on the driver's side. I got my knife out and leaned in to reach him until my head and shoulders were in the car. I brought the knife across his face. When he covered up I stabbed him twice in the left shoulder and twice in the thigh. By this time Nicky was pulling me out of the car. We drove away and left him.

Right after that Johnny was sent away to Deer Island for a time. His wife came down and wanted to pay off his loan. I refused.

"Look," I said, "your husband is in jail and I don't take money like that. You need it for your bills. Just make sure he pays what he borrowed from me when he gets out."

A few weeks later, Johnny Revere came to see me. He had a scar three inches long from his lip to his cheek. I settled the debt for $800 and was well rid of him. As he left, I said: "I didn't want to stab you and I don't get my jollies doing things like that, but I told you not to hassle me or you'd get stabbed."

Johnny Revere said: "I don't blame you. It was my fault."

I was glad he said it because when I hurt a customer I always wanted to make sure it was their fault.

8

Business could be fun as well as violent. Especially the arson business. There was this restaurant out in the Wellesley area. It was giving its competitor across the street too much competition, so the competitor paid us $2,000 to burn it down. When it reopened months later, we got another $2,000 to burn it down again.

Another job was a meat store in the Haymarket area. It only paid $600. Then there was a guy with a garage on Bremen Street in East Boston. He wanted to expand so he paid $500 to have the empty house on the lot next door burned down. We obliged. A guy named Skinny who had a bar on Day Square paid $1,000 to have it burned so he could collect the insurance. We totaled it. Even the floor caved in. Out in Gloucester was a book store. We got $1,000 to burn it.

Leo Swartz owned a cafe in Jamaica Plains. A cop opened a cafe down the street. Leo gave me $500 to throw a couple of stink bombs in the cop's joint. When the smell hit, the customers took off.

Everybody had an angle and there was always plenty of money for the guy willing to do what somebody wanted done. Hell, there was even a nut to take the rap for the Boston Strangler. The nut's name was Albert DeSalvo, but that's another story.

Connie Frizzi came up with a real cute caper that had nothing to do with arson. He found out that Ben Tilly had left a suitcase full of a stolen coin collection with the manager of a shoe store in Cambridge. The guy was to hold it until Tilly came back. It was worth a cool $10,000.

We drove over to the shoe store on a dark, rainy day. Connie waited in the car around the corner while I went into the store and asked for the manager by name. He was a tall man with glasses and grayish hair.

"Can I help you?" he said. I said:

"Ben told me to pick up the suitcase."

The manager stiffened. "I don't know what you mean."

I said: "Listen, don't hassle me. Ben has a buyer down at the Iron Horse in North Station and the buyer's got to catch a plane back to New York in an hour. I haven't got much time."

The manager said: "But I don't know you."

I said: "How the hell do you think I know about the coins? If I go back to the meet Ben has and the buyer's gone, I'll come back and break this fucking store up with your head. Give me the god-damned suitcase and stop playing Dick Tracy with me, you asshole."

The manager said: "All right."

He gave it to me and I said: "Ben knows what was in here so if there's any coins missing you're in trouble."

I walked out and couldn't find Connie Frizzi. After I had walked three blocks with that heavy suitcase, he pulled around the corner. I said: "You pea-hearted asshole, why did you come at all? I ought to keep the whole suitcase."

Connie said: "I didn't want to have my license number taken."

"Yeah," I said. "You sure think of Connie and to fuck with me."

That suitcase had rolls and rolls of coins: dollars, quarters, nickels, dimes, pennies and some foreign coins. We sold the collection fast for $5,000. I often wondered what happened when Ben went back and asked for the suitcase.

Things didn't always work out so well. Take the time Russell Saia came to me with a BIG idea. Saia handled hot cars mostly, selling a lot of them up in Canada, but he was a steady customer of mine. Paid vig on $1,500. One day he came to me and said: "My girlfriend works in a bank. She stole seven blank checks—bank checks. Take me to see Henry Tameleo and you get a piece of everything I get."

I took him to see Henry and Henry was interested. The checks were cashed one at a time by big businessmen and the money was deposited in a bank in the Bahamas. By the time the seventh check was cashed there was over $400,000 in that bank. My end was $75,000.

Something went wrong though. The law got on to the fact that the checks were bogus and traced the money to the Bahamas. The law was waiting to see who would collect it. Nobody did. You might say the law stole the whole boat ride from us.

Well, you win a few and lose a few. Take the time Jumbo Chiampa, Tony Brazzo and a guy called Yogi came to me with a proposition we be partners in a crap game. Jumbo had this club on the first floor of a house his family owned, and the door already had one-way glass in it.

They wanted me to raise a $3,000 bank. I told them I could get the money by agreeing to pay back $600 a week for six weeks. Actually, I drove into town and then came back and gave them the $3,000 out of my own shylock.

We set up tables with sides to bounce the dice off, and fixed up the joint the way it should be. The first night we made $2,600 and the second night the score was $1,500. It paid me back $3,600 that we were supposed to owe. Actually, I had made $600 and was a 25 percent partner. It looked good. We were out of debt and had a $3,500 kitty.

The very next night we blew it all. Everybody left and we were sitting around talking about it when we got word this vice squad detective was going to raid us. I said: "It sure didn't take him long to find out."

But it was Mickey the Wise Guy who showed up next morning instead. He had three men with him. Mickey the Wise Guy said: "The Office wants you to close this game."

Jumbo said: "It's closed now, but if you'd come by yesterday morning we'd still have thirty-five hundred dollars."

3

The Old Fox

As 1965 began, Joe [Barboza] Baron was edging closer to participation in the gang war which was growing in size and intensity. Friendship for Jimmy "the Bear" Flemmi, and respect for Buddy McLean, whom he had met in prison, were the factors responsible. Self-interest, however, suggested a working relationship with the Office would be more profitable. Despite a crippling shortage of Mafia "soldiers" to enforce his will, Raymond Patriarca from his shabby office in Providence was trying to expand his power in divided Boston. The situation spelled opportunity for Joe if he could stay alive long enough to grasp it. Meanwhile, it was business as usual—for Joe and everyone else.

1

Chico and I were talking about how Buddy McLean had a soft heart beneath his thick hide. Chico had his doubts so I reminded him of Willie Delaney's death last August.

Willie was a friend of Harold Hannon, and that's why he got into trouble. Hannon was a McLaughlin man. Back after Buddy killed Bernie McLaughlin, Hannon drove around town with Georgie McLaughlin hidden in the car trunk and looking out a peephole for a chance to shoot McLean.

Naturally, when McLean heard about it he wasn't very happy. It took a little while to arrange, but a girl set Hannon up. He arrived at his apartment for a date, bringing Willie along with him. Buddy and some other people were inside. They grabbed Hannon and Willie, handcuffed them, and used a blow torch held near Hannon's balls to make him talk. He talked, and then he was killed.

Willie was told that he was going to get it too. After all, he had been warned to stay away from Hannon. But Buddy didn't have anything personal against Willie. It just isn't good policy to leave unfriendly witnesses alive. So he let Willie have a fifth of booze and ten seconals, and when Willie had passed out they quietly strangled him and dropped him and Hannon into the river.

Chico was still arguing about it when the Bear called and asked me to come over to Dearborn Square on a matter involving money. We drove over. The Bear got into the back seat next to Chico and said: "Bobby Rasmussen is trying to shake down some of the Plymouth mail robbers. Red and Aggie just offered me a fifteen thousand dollar contract on him. You interested?"

I wasn't interested and said so. Free-lance killing isn't my bag. Chico said: "Man, I could use the bread. I'll whack him out with you, Bear."

I said: "Listen, if you want to use Chico it's all right by me. I suppose you've got the spot picked out."

"Not really," said the Bear. "The offer is only a few hours old. Wimpy and I just came back from seeing them."

"Well, you and Chico work it out," I said. "I've got to go chase that asshole Nutilly down. He's seven weeks behind in his payments."

"All right," said the Bear. "I'll see you down at the Ebbtide tonight."

Nick drove me off and we looked for Nutilly on Friend Street. But the Bear didn't show up that night at the Ebbtide.

In fact it was three days later before I saw him. He told us the contract was off. Red and Aggie had decided to handle it themselves. The Bear seemed a little disappointed but Chico took it with a shrug.

A few days passed and the newspapers had another headline murder. Wimpy Bennett told me what happened.

It seems that Rasmussen was really uptight for money. So Aggie took him to an apartment in Water town. Aggie said it was a bookie's pad and that the bookie kept all his money in the safe until the end of each week. It just so happened, Aggie said, that he had duplicated the keys to the apartment and had somehow acquired the combination of the safe. They opened the safe which was in a closet and looked in the cashbox. There was $2,700 in the box, but Aggie said to leave it alone. Later in the week there'd be a lot more—maybe ten thousand dollars. Bobby was happy to wait.

The night Aggie and Rasmussen returned to the apartment, a slight change had occurred. The carpet, tables and chairs had all been covered with plastic, and inside the apartment was an ex-baseball player with a bat in his hand. Aggie opened the door and politely stood aside to let Rasmussen enter. The baseball player swung his bat and swung it again and again. Then they carried the body to the car. Aggie went back and collected all the sheets of plastic which had caught the blood. They drove a good distance from Watertown and dumped Bobby Rasmussen from the car. The baseball player got out and fired a bullet into Bobby's head, and that was that.

"So they did take care of it themselves," I said.

"Yeah," Wimpy said. "They couldn't afford to let somebody else straighten it out because they would have been sitting ducks for the people who straightened it out."

"The Bear must have been scheming with the same thought," I said. "No wonder he wanted to do it so badly."

Wimpy was a good conversationalist. One day we were standing on the square talking and he said: "Joe, want to make fifteen hundred dollars?"

I said: "I'm always game."

Wimpy said: "Johnny Murray shot this dude a few days ago in an apartment in the South End. He told his brother to get rid of the body, and he left. He came back yesterday and the body was still there. His brother froze up and left the stiff there."

"I don't want no part of it," I said. "Too many people know about it by now."

Within a couple of days the newspapers had a story about a body found cut up in sections and stashed in three suitcases left in the alley outside a downtown hotel. It was rather decomposed, leading the cops to believe it had been dead for some time.

Johnny Murray was later shot by Wimpy.

Wimpy made believe he was sleeping in the back of this car that his partner was driving. Murray was in the front seat. Suddenly Wimpy sat up and shot Johnny in the back of the head. Who the hell knows why? Wimpy isn't around any more.

2

I was at the Ebbtide with Henry Tameleo, Ronnie Casesso, Romeo Martin, Chico and Nicky. It was early in the evening and the place was still quiet. In through the back door came three guys. The tall one with the suit on looked familiar. He waved to me, and then I knew who it was. It was Stevie Hughes. He had lost fifty pounds since I last saw him at Walpole. I had met him in the boxing room and he had told me he liked the way I fought.

Stevie looked real good after losing all that weight. He now weighed about 175, and had wide shoulders, a trim waist and jet black hair. He came over to the table with the two guys and introduced them. One was his brother, Connie Hughes, and the other was Maxie Shackelford. We all shook hands and they sat down. I signaled Chico to call Dearborn Square and I told Romeo to get some guns out of the cellar just in case.

Now Stevie didn't know I was a sympathizer for the McLean side and growing more involved because of the Bear. The war had broken up a lot of friendships but it wouldn't break mine. Stevie and, Tommy Ballou had been friends but when Punchie McLaughlin tried to make Tommy come in on his side, Tommy went over to McLean while Stevie stayed with Punchie. Sitting there in the Ebbtide I thought about it.

It wasn't long before Wimpy Bennett, the Bear, his brother Stevie and Frank Salami came in and joined up. We put tables together to make room. Henry Tameleo had mysteriously drifted off—the Office was officially neutral and Henry didn't want to get in the line of fire. Richie Castucci was walking around nervously. He kept wringing his hands and glancing at us. Eddie Miami was down with the others in the front section of the restaurant.

Stevie Hughes said: "I want to make peace with Buddy McLean. If Buddy gives his word, I'll accept it."

The Bear said: "I'll talk to Buddy and do my best. If this war keeps up, who knows how many people sitting here tonight will die?"

The Bear was just talking, but five people sitting there were to die in the war and he was to be seriously wounded.

Hughes said: "All I want to do now is make money."

There was some small talk, and Hughes and his party left. The Bear carried the peace offer to McLean. Buddy was furious. He said: "I don't want no peace with him because he is a lying sneaking weasel. The only peace we'll ever get between us is when one of us is dead."

3

Henry Tameleo and I were sitting at a table in the restaurant part of the Ebbtide. The restaurant was about six steps above the level of the dance floor and an oval bar. Behind the restaurant was a hallway which led to a back entrance and also connected to the coatroom. There was a hidden door in the coat room which led to a secret office and in the secret office was another door leading to yet another office.

Henry said: "Let's go in the back office. I want to talk to you."

We went into the coatroom and there I saw Vinnie "the Pig" Teresa. Teresa was a big slob who sometimes drove Henry around, but basically he was a con-man. Once he conned some of Henry's friends into cashing $1,800 worth of bad checks. Henry asked me to do something to teach him a lesson. I caught him at Arthur's Farm and worked him over. Well, today, Vinnie was playing the big shot with this girl named Dusty. He had her backed up against the wall, her blouse torn open and her bra pushed up over her chest. Vinnie was panting and trying to grab her titty, and she was fighting to get away.

Henry just looked at Vinnie, glanced at me and went on into the secret office. I shoved Teresa into the coat racks. He tumbled over and began yelling: "Please, Joe, don't hit me." I kicked him in the side and he crawled out of the coatroom on his knees. I took Dusty into the first secret office and told her to straighten herself out. Then I went into the back office where Henry was waiting. He didn't even mention Teresa. Instead, he said: "I got two members on the Revere License Board in my pocket. Now all I need is one more to control it."

"Beautiful," I said.

"If I can get control, I'll make the concessions on the beach pay a thousand or more to open. If they don't pay, I'll pull their license and sell them to the suckers waiting in line. They'll have to kickback monthly too, of course. You can have a piece of it, Joe."

With the Office it never paid to seem too greedy so I just said: "I don't need it, Henry. Give my piece to Raymond as a gift from me."

Henry said: "Joe, I wish you'd get to hell out of this war. Raymond and I can get you a good job in Vegas. You'll make a good week's pay."

I said: "Henry, I've got to stay by the Bear."

Henry said: "Think about it, Joe. Now the guy I'm trying to move on the license board works as a baker in Lynn. I want you to slap him around but I don't want no marks. Go down there with a couple of the boys and scare him good. If I get him I'll milk them dry on this beach."

The next day after finding where to go, I went down with Ronnie Casesso, Freddie Chiampa and Chico. The bakery, painted white, was on the corner. There was a back entrance on a side street so we parked on the side street. Chico said: "See that drugstore on the corner? Pineapple Stevenson works there for T.L."

I said: "Tony Lombardi is a piece of shit. I'll bet he gives Wesley ice water and crabs for working there." "Is that Pineapple's name?" asked Chico. "Wesley?"

I said: "Yeah. Wesley taught me a lot in the gym. He'd be one of the best fighters in Boston if he'd only train right."

Chiampa said: "T.L. has a helluva book action and shylock business in that drugstore."

I said: "Yeah. The yellow slob kicks back to the Office for protection. He buys his balls."

We got out of the car. I had a sash weight up my sleeve. We all went in the back way with our coat collars turned up and our hat lids pulled down over our sunglasses. It was all very simple. I asked one of the employees where the boss was. He looked at me with frightened eyes and said he didn't know. I dropped the sash weight accidentally on purpose to the floor and then picked it up hurriedly with a great pretense of hiding it. The guy just stared, his mouth wide open, and we left.

That evening Henry told me: "After you left, the man called up frightened and asked for my help. I told him I'd help him if he was with me. He said he'd do anything I wanted. So now I control the license board in Revere."

4

It was some time in February, 1965, and my blue convertible with the gold roof was parked on the street. I was across the street in an old house that was the Bear's afterhours joint. Actually it looked like the Bear's haunted house, painted smoky gray like it was. The front door screeched when you entered. Upon entering you were in a dim hallway. Immediately to the right was a large parlor with a bar. It was anything but class. There were hookers, pimps, thieves, bookies, hit men—you name it—in a black and white mixture. The room on your left had tables and chairs and a jukebox. The wallpaper was peeling and the ceiling was cracked. Down the hall was a brightly lit room where a card game was going on and beyond that was still another cardroom. Looking straight ahead was another room that if you walked in you fell through the floor.

I was leaning against the wall in the cardroom watching the Bear playing a hundred dollars a hand on blackjack. I was furious for him and sad too. Furious at the way he gambled his money, and sad because he was losing. After a time, Nicky and I left. When we got to the sidewalk a car pulled up and a voice said: "Hey, Joe."

It was a law car. I ran back inside and hid my gun. Nicky, that fat bastard, kept walking, trying to shake his gun down his leg but his leg was so fat the gun couldn't pass. When he sat down in the car, however, it fell out and landed near the gas pedal. The detective grabbed it and handcuffed Nicky and put him in side his car. At that point, I came back out. The detective said: "Why did you run?"

I said: "I couldn't see who it was in the car."

He said: "You had a gun."

I said: "Who? Me? No, man."

The detective said: "Well, we got Nicky with a gun in your car."

I said: "Illegal search."

He said: "Makes no difference. The boss said if it don't stick it'll cost you plenty between bail and attorney fees."

I looked at Nicky sitting in the back of the car and felt bad because he had the gun to protect me. He was getting into the gang war for me just like I was getting in for the Bear. Now this detective I'd known for a long time and once he had promised to help me if I ever needed anything. Well, I needed something now. I said: "You know that kid is in that car for me. He was carrying that gun for me. Give him a break."

He said: "Joe, it's too late. Wimpy and Peter Paulos are watching across the street. If I let Nicky go they'll tell Frank Stuart and he'll run it back to the station."

I said: "I'm asking you now, begging you, to do me the favor and let him go."

He said: "Let me speak to my partner."

He came back and said: "Look, we'll take you both down to the station because you got smart mouth, see, and then we'll let you go. Don't say nothing about the gun. I'll see you in East Boston tomorrow and you'll give me one hundred dollars."

I said: "Man, I sure won't forget this. Thanks." We went down to the station and they let us go and we took a cab back to the car. Nicky left me off at my home. I said: "I'll see you tomorrow, Dr. Zorba." I called him Dr. Zorba because he reminded me of a quack who used to scheme and figure things to perfection but never got nothing right.

I met the detective next day and give him his money. I was sincerely grateful for he could've asked for $2,500 and got it. About five nights later, Peter Paulos called me up and said: "So and so wants to see you down at the station."

"How come?" Peter said: "He heard you paid two hundred to the law to hush up what happened the other night. Don't worry about it; I just gave him fifty dollars."

Well, I figured the officer had wanted his cut and got it, but I still had to go down. When I got there they sat me down and officially asked the question. I went into my act. I said: "Sir, I've been in trouble all my life and went to prison for petty things less serious than carrying a gun. I wish I could buy my way out of such situations, but I know I can't and this is a credit to the fine officers that serve under you."

He said: "All right, that's all. Thank you."

5

Sometime in May, 1965, I was sitting in the Ebbtide at Revere. It was about 9 P.M. Richie Castucci, Eddie Miami, Bobby Cardillo, Romeo Martin, Nicky and Chico were there along with a lot of other people. Castucci answered the phone and came back and said: "Joe, you want to make a thousand dollars?"

I said: "Is Chinese arithmetic hard?"

Richie said: "Junior Ventola is at a theater on Washington Street seeing a movie. He just spotted his ex-girlfriend and the guy that took her away. I'll pay you a thousand if you'll go in there and bust his face up."

I thought about Junior and the girl. After Henry Tameleo bought Junior out, he started coming to the Ebbtide with this girl. She was a singer and had a good voice and sometimes sang at the Ebbtide just for kicks. Somewhere along the line this guy started making a play for her. The chick started to respond. Junior went into his Bogart gangster bag and told the dude "to hook it and get in the wind." That caused the dude and the girl to get into the wind together and to blow. Junior was sore and said he'd get even. I was still cold with Junior because of the trouble I'd had with him, but $1,000 was interesting. I said okay.

The other guys and I talked and it was decided that Chico, Romeo, Cardillo and I would go. Even split. Romeo said he had a bat in his car and would hit the dude with it. That was all right with me. I wasn't going to hit no dude with a bat for $250.

We went in Romeo's car. On the way, I said: "We'll go in and as soon as the Shit comes out, I'll go back to the car and get it going. I'll be the wheelman."

All the guys knew that "the Shit" was my name for Junior.

I parked at the back entrance in an alley leading to Fremont Street. We went in and found Junior at the men's room. All the while I was in the theater I had a handkerchief to my mouth and nose, covering my face. I coughed a lot too. Junior pointed out the dude sitting in the center aisle in the middle of the row.

When the commotion started I was standing near the downward ramp ready to go out the rear exit. Romeo went up the row of seats saying "Excuse me, excuse me, excuse me." Then, THOCK, he hit the dude in the face with the bat and THOCK, another in the head. Women started screaming, one fainted, and the lights went on. I was down the ramp with another coughing fit and Chico was with me because I didn't want him sticking his neck out for no $250. We ran out and got the car started but I kept the lights off. Romeo and Cardillo came. I drove out the alley with the lights still off, took a left on Fremont, took a right up the hill to Beacon Street. Halfway up the hill I put the lights on.

We got the bread when we got back to the Ebbtide. I was Junior's friend for life. The story was never in the papers.

From then on I was always paranoid in theaters.

6

I was down on Prince Street in the North End. Prince Street was no different from three-fourths of the North End which is an Italian ghetto. The buildings were run-down; the narrow streets were congested with cars, vendors, people; the air smelled of imported cheese, bread and pastries. In spite of its dismal looking buildings, all holding each other up, and the smell of decay, the North End was never a lonely place. Children were playing and yelling. People were leaning out of their windows or sitting on fire escapes, all talking. Italian immigrants stood in front of the coffee shops and Wise Guys stood in front of bars and old stores converted into clubs. They wore silk mohair suits and diamonds on their pinkies.

Peter Limone came out of the Dog House. The Dog House was the daytime office of Jerry Anguilo, the head man in Boston for Raymond Patriarca who was supposed to be the Mafia boss of New England. His office was in Providence, Rhode Island.

Peter said: "I want to talk to you, Joe."

I said: "Yeah, Peter, what's on your mind?" "

A lot of our people have been complaining about Deegan killing the Sacramoni kid," Peter said. "Also, Deegan was the one that robbed Popollo's house and grabbed $82,000 of action money that belongs to the Office."

I knew all about it. Deegan, an ex-boxer, broke into the home of a bookie named Popollo. With him was Statopoulos, the Greek, and a kid named Ricco Sacramoni. The Office was mad and wanted to find out who did it. Deegan got scared and came up with a wild idea like most ideas born out of desperation. He thought if he killed someone the Office would think twice before hassling him. But who was to be the victim? The opportunity came when Deegan had an argument with Sacramoni over some pills. Deegan and

Sacramoni were in a car with Statopoulos when it happened.

Statopoulos had told me: "I never wanted it to happen," he said. "Teddy stuck him with a knife in the car and later shot him. I sure felt terrible over it."

So I told Peter Limone: "Yeah, I heard that."

"Do you think you can handle the Deegan problem?" asked Peter.

I said: "Let me speak to Henry first."

"I'll give you $7,500 if you can get it done," Peter said.

We talked some more about it and then I left. Later, I saw Henry Tameleo at the Ebbtide in Revere. Henry was Raymond's right hand man and I trusted him.

I said to him: "Peter wants me to handle the Deegan situation."

Henry said: "Yes, it's okay. He has to go."

"I'll take care of it right after I get back from Florida," I said.

As I was driving home after talking to Henry, I thought about it. I had no idea how I was going to do it, but I knew if I handled it right I wouldn't have no more worries about the Office moving in on my shylock business. I was now making $4,000 a week and life was real good with that pay. I was enjoying it which is why I was going to Florida. Henry had made arrangements for Ronnie Casesso to have somebody meet me at the airport and I had reservations at the Cadillac Hotel under the name of Baron. When the day came for me to fly to Florida, I really felt good. It was in the middle of the winter and I was leaving the cold, snow and ice of New England for the warm, sunny beaches of Florida. Yes, I thought, not bad for a Portugee named Barboza from New Bedford.

When the plane landed, Bobby Vincent, a legit kid from Boston, picked me up and took me to the hotel. Next day Ronnie came up to my room and we shook hands. He wanted me to move in at the house he was renting for $1,000 a month. Ronnie and I hit it off great together and got along so well we agreed to go into partnership together. One day we were standing outside the Peppermint Lounge talking and a dark green car pulled up and out stepped Louie Grieco in a black raincoat, dark sun glasses and wearing black gloves. I went over to his car and said, "Hey! Hi, Louie."

He said: "Hi," and looked troubled.

"What's bothering you?" I said.

We walked over to the side of the Peppermint and around the corner of the building so they couldn't hear us. Louie said: "The reason why I don't want to go near those guys is because of that guy Hymie sitting there with Toto and Ronnie. I slapped him in the mouth."

Grieco had once been a heavyweight fighter. He was about fifty and weighed about 260 pounds. Had ape-like features and manner. Walked with a slight limp from a wound he got in the Philippines during the Second World War. Had a reputation as being a hit man for the Office."

"What you looking so depressed about?" I asked. He said: "That fucking wife of mine has been going out with some dude and she's going to swear out a warrant for me and I'm on probation in this state."

He stopped a minute and then he said: "Joe, do me a favor and kill her. I'll return the favor anyway you want it."

"I got a contract I got to put together," I said.

Louie said: "Who is it?"

"Teddy Deegan, but I haven't solved it yet."

Louie said: "Will you let me in on it? I need the money bad. Roy French is friendly with Deegan and I'm friendly with Roy. Maybe I can talk Roy into setting Teddy up."

The idea was a sound one. "Okay," I said. "You'll get the same equal share as the other people involved. Fair enough?"

Louie said: "Yeh."

"I'm going back to Boston right away because I want to get going on this thing," I said.

Louie said, "I'll be back soon and we'll get together and speak to Roy."

Louie left and I went back to Ronnie and Toto and Hymie. As we were driving back to Ronnie's house, Ronnie said: "I got to break into a house tonight for Toto."

He showed me a small bottle of blue and white capsules and then he said: "They're asthma pills but these are filled with poison. I'm going to switch these with the ones the guy keeps in his medicine cabinet."

"What a move," I said. "You never know."

Then Ronnie told me about how he and Romeo walked right into the home of singer Buddy Greco and his wife. Buddy's wife had almost nothing on and Romeo wanted to rape her but they took the jewelry and money and then left.

A day or two later I left to go back to Boston. Ronnie didn't want me to go back. Then he said: "Fuck Florida! I was supposed to stay here till March but I won't. I'll follow you back in about a week."

When I got back to Logan Airport, Chico and Nicky picked me up and drove me to my apartment in Chelsea on the Parkway. Several days passed and Louie Grieco came back and we went down to the Ebbtide in Revere to speak to Roy French. Roy went for it after I told him I'd talk to Buddy McLean. Roy was a friend of Georgie McLaughlin, you see, and had hid Georgie for awhile at his home when Buddy was looking for Georgie. Buddy had sent word that Roy was siding with the McLaughlins in the gang war, and Roy was paranoid about it. So he was somewhat relieved when I said I'd talk to Buddy, and he promised he'd get in touch with Deegan.

Several days went by and then Roy told me that he had met with Deegan and Statopoulos the Greek and the three of them had decided to pull a burglary of a finance company in Chelsea. The finance company was on the second floor. The rear door to the finance company would be left open. I saw

Peter Limone and he said he'd add $2,500 for Statopoulos. Henry said it was okay with him so I told Ronnie the situation. Ronnie wanted in.

I said: "We need at least four people."

Ronnie said: "Romeo will want in."

"Look, Ronnie," I said. "This is an Office contract. The Office is to know only that you and I did it."

The night of the hit we were in the Ebbtide: Ronnie, Romeo, Joe "the Horse" Salvati and Chico. Outside, waiting down the street in his car, was Louie Grieco. We were all waiting for Deegan to call Roy and tell him he was coming to pick up Roy for the finance company job. The call finally came. Ronnie, Joe "the Horse" and I went out the back door to Romeo's car. I put on a bullet-proof vest, false mustache and plain-glass glasses. Ronnie put on a phony mustache and phony horn-rimmed glasses. The Horse put on a bald-headed wig. Chico took the car he had and drove to the street where the alley went down behind the finance company. He parked up the street where he could make a fast right and stall the car if the law came. It was a legit car and no law was broken if his car stalled and blocked the law from passing. Romeo went in Louie's car with Louie. Their job was to be in the alley when Roy came with Deegan. They were to shoot Deegan and run back to the car and drive back to the Ebbtide. Louie would leave them there and drive off and I'd see him the next day when I got the money.

Ronnie, the Horse and I were going to take care of the Greek who was supposed to come in his own car and be the lookout while Roy and Deegan pulled the job. We were to park on Broadway across the street from the alley. When we saw the Greek pull up, Ronnie and I were to get out of the car and stand on the corner. When we heard shots inside the alley we would run to the Greek's car. I had a .357 magnum that would penetrate the door of the car if I couldn't get a clear shot at the Greek. In the meantime, the Horse would unzipper the rear window of the convertible and then get in the front seat and start the car. He would then open both doors of the car and get in the middle of the front seat and pull it forward so Ronnie could jump in the back and stick the .30 caliber carbine out the rear window to cover anybody that followed us. I would jump in front and drive because I was familiar with Chelsea because I lived there.

That's how it was supposed to happen, anyway.

We drove to where we were supposed to be and we watched Romeo and Louie go into the alley to wait for Roy and Deegan. I bent the front plate of the car so no numbers would show and Ronnie bent the rear plate leaving three numbers exposed. I had the wheels turned completely toward the street so that all I had to do when the time came was to step on the gas and the car would be out of the slot into the middle of the one-way street.

"What does this motherfucker want?" I said.

The man was wearing a topcoat and a soft hat and he was standing on the sidewalk looking at the front of the car. He walked by and then came back to the window where I was sitting and said: "Hey, your plate is bent."

I got a weird feeling. This dude was a detective. So I pulled out fast, took a right on Broadway and then the next left. I stopped and let Ronnie out. He was to get the guys out of the alley before Roy arrived with Deegan. I raced back to the Ebbtide.

After awhile they came in. The first one I saw was Roy. He said: "It's done."

I said: "You got blood on your shoes."

He said: "I'll take care of it." Ronnie gave me his story. He said: "When I went back to tell them, the Greek's car pulled up and I had to sit with Chico. I saw them go into the alley. Then Statopoulos' car came shooting by me. I saw the boys come out of the alley and get into their car so Chico and I left."

Louie said: "I was in the alley when the first shot was fired. I stepped out and Deegan was down so I fired at his body."

Romeo said: "I was inside the door to the finance company when I heard the shots. I stepped out and saw Deegan so I put the gun close to his head and fired again to make sure."

That left it up to Roy. He said: "We drove to the alley. Deegan only had a screwdriver. The Greek didn't have anything. When we went into the alley I got scared I'd get caught in a crossfire so I shot Teddy in the head first. When I left the alley the Greek was still in his car. I couldn't figure what had happened to you so I waved my hand for him to leave and he took off in the car."

The next day I went to see Peter Limone. He said: "That's one less Irish motherfucker," and gave me the $7,500. Ronnie and I got credit for the hit. And then I got word that the man wanted to meet us in Rhode Island.

Ronnie and the Bear went with me. When we got to the Federal Hill section of Providence we parked in the Roman Gardens' parking lot and went across the street for a quick breakfast. It was around 11 o'clock in the morning. Henry Tameleo got word we were there and he came in and had a cup of coffee. Then we went to Raymond's office. It was an old store on the corner that had been converted to a pinball and cigarette vending machine business. Back of the store on the left hand side was a partition and back of it was an office about twelve feet wide and twenty feet long. The place was far from classy, more poor than rich, but when people spoke of "the Office" this is what they meant.

Henry said: "This is Joe Barboza."

I said: "My pleasure, Mr. Patriarca."

The man said: "Call me Raymond."

He was a medium built man with straight, combed-back black hair, piercing eyes and hawk-like features. His mouth was shaped like a lizard's mouth and had a purple look to it. I suspected him of a heart condition, but I found out later it was because of his diabetic condition. He was wearing a dark blue suit and white socks. On his finger he wore a white gold ring with four diamonds in a line. Each diamond was a carat or more.

We left after about an hour. On the way to Boston the Bear said: "You didn't have much to say in there. What were you thinking?"

I said: "I was thinking how I could bite his finger off and get that diamond ring."

The Bear and Ronnie started laughing.

I said: "What the fuck is funny?"

7

While I liked Henry Tameleo, Ronnie and some of the other dudes connected with the Office, I never let my relationship with Raymond blind me as to how things stood. As with others in the gang war, all dealings with the Office were matters of business. We were independent operators, not Mafia "soldiers" who took some blood oath and were bound by a code of *omerta*. For that matter, I never thought the blood oath did anybody any good if Raymond decided they were too hot for *his* health.

Buddy McLean and Howie Winters were regular visitors to Raymond's office in Rhode Island, informing him of events concerning the gang war, business deals and the like. Other people who went up there often were Wimpy Bennett, the Bear and his brother, Frank Salanni, Freddie Chiampa, Ronnie Casesso. Ronnie was the only one who was a member of the Mafia, but he was under Joe Anselmo who ran Chelsea and other suburban towns.

Every week Jerry Anguilo, Larry Biaoni, Peter Limone and other men connected with the Office would go see

Raymond and spread lies about us independents. Call it jealousy or fear, but they knocked us continuously. But Raymond didn't get where he was for nothing. He created this relationship with us independents purposely to keep a tighter hold on his members. He expected this kind of talk from his members. He wanted this relationship so he could call on the seventy-five of us any time the members stepped out of line. He kept the members in check by having seventy-five independents who showed respect to the members but would never get close to them. The members knew that if Raymond told us to whack out one of the members, we independents would do it gladly. This knowledge kept the members in constant fear.

At one meeting I attended, Raymond said of his members: "They did something ten years ago and they figure they don't have to do anything but play centerfield for the rest of their lives."

Another time he got mad at Romeo Martin who was bragging that he had gone to New York and killed two people for Raymond. It wasn't so. Raymond told me: "Joe, supposing by coincidence two guys did get killed in New York at the time this fool is running his mouth. What could I say to the boys in New York? I'd be in trouble."

I noticed Raymond's lips were more purple than usual. Some time later Romeo was hit. I never did find out who killed him—there were so many guys after him—but Raymond was very satisfied. Romeo was found in a car in Revere with four bullets in his head, one through his neck, five dum dum bullets in his chest and one in his arm. Whoever killed him did a good job.

One day the subject of the gang war came up at Raymond's office. Somebody mentioned Georgie McLaughlin. Raymond said: "That little asshole has done nothing for two years but hide and cost his friends money. I'm going to sit him in that chair in front of you guys and tell him to forget this beef and stop the war. If he says no, then you can kill him right in that chair."

I guess we didn't look convinced or something because Raymond continued: "This war has got to get over with, one way or another, even if I have to declare martial law. It's costing too much money. We can't operate properly."

Wimpy said: "If you can get them to stop trying to kill us, we'll stop our side. But how can you trust the word of that sick little bastard, Georgie McLaughlin?"

Raymond said: "I'm going to call him up here and speak to him. I've called him to come in four or five times now, but he won't come. He don't trust me no more."

I thought: "Sure, he don't trust you, Raymond. You had Nazzarin killed after he worked for you for years. Georgie worked for you and now you want him killed. Nobody means nothing to you, you cold-blooded bastard."

And the gang war went on.

4

The Big Kill

Even as the gang war approached its bloody climax, Joe found himself facing new danger from Mafia members jealous of his friendly relationship with Raymond Patriarca and fearful of his prowess as a killer. Barboza wasn't dismayed, however. He still had friends and he still had confidence in himself. So long as the independents were united under the strong leadership of Buddy McLean, neither the McLaughlins or the Mafia could match them. But Joe was human, and sometimes even his gun jammed at the wrong moment.

1

I was up at the Tap Royal in the Winter Hill section of Somerville, and, of course, I was talking about the gang war with Buddy McLean. Buddy was a little upset about the way the McLaughlins were getting secret aid from some punks who pretended to be neutral. Buddy said: "We spoke to Charlie Brown at the Frolics about helping the Hughes brothers and he swore he'd never get involved again, yet that lying punk is still helping them. He's fencing their hot merchandise from that store of his in Chelsea."

Connie and Stevie Hughes were the McLaughlins' chief allies and Buddy wanted them almost as bad as he wanted Punchie and Georgie.

I said: "I go by his place every day. I'll have a talk with him."

Buddy said: "Watch out when you go by there. Don't let the Hughes brothers catch you flat-footed."

I said: "In that case I'll put spotters on the store."

"Good," said Buddy. "See what you can do. Maybe you'll scare the guy off."

That night I walked into Charlie Brown's store. Nicky and Chico were with me. He had the front windows blocked off with advertisements so you couldn't see in. He was behind the counter when I came in. I had on a black mohair topcoat with a black velvet collar, a green mohair suit, a black tailormade hat made from beaver skins by Harry the Hatter in Lynn, black pigskin gloves with no lining and a pair of wrap-around sunglasses.

I said: "Charlie, I ain't coming in here but once. Do you understand?"

As I spoke, I slammed my coat pocket against the counter. The thud left no doubt I had a gun in my pocket. Charlie Brown turned pale.

He said: "Man, I don't know what you're talking about."

I said: "Of course you don't. You do remember Buddy McLean grabbing you down at the Frolics, don't you?"

"Well, yeah," said Charlie.

I made my voice into a growl: "That warning wasn't good enough, was it? Cause you're still fucking around with the Hughes, selling their hot stuff and mailing them money."

"No, no," stammered Charlie.

"Don't lie to me, you weasel."

"Please believe me," said Charlie Brown.

"Look," I said. "As long as you feed them guys money, they can buy guns to use against us when they come out of the woodwork. They can stay off the streets where we can't get them. Understand?"

"I know what you mean," said Charlie.

"It's up to you, Charlie," I said. "This is your last warning. Do you read me?"

"Yes," said Charlie. I left with Nicky and Chico. We drove up to see Buddy. He was more elated than I expected. He hugged me. I didn't think it was that important, but apparently he did.

Two weeks passed. I went to the Continental Restaurant on the Pike. It was the first time I'd been there and I was impressed. I'm a fanatic about good food and the Continental ranked with the best. I wore a blue silk mohair suit with no belt, so when I went in I left my gun under the car seat. When I came out, full and happy, I was too lazy to get it out from under the seat.

When I got to my apartment, I took the babysitter to her house and then drove on through Chelsea to Charlie Brown's store. When I came to his store he was standing out front. He looked away as if he hadn't seen my car, but I was sure he had. He had to know my car. The law called it "Barboza's James Bond car." It was a 1965 luxury sedan, an Oldsmobile with a starfire motor and all the accessories plus a few extras like an alarm system, a device for making smoke screens and so forth.

I stared in the mirror looking back at Brown and was still looking when I had to stop for a red light at the corner. In the mirror I noticed a white car pull around the street from beside Brown's store. It came up behind me and stopped twenty feet away. I reached for my gun under the seat as he stopped. A guy in a cap and blue coveralls got out. He had a gun in his hand. I stepped on the gas and shot through the red light. Then I took a left by the police station. The white car went straight ahead at a fast rate of speed. I figured he planned to intercept me at the Chelsea-East Boston Bridge, so I turned around and went back the way I had come. Then I went over to Revere and called Freddie Chiampa to meet me at the Surf Club. As I had it figured, Charlie Brown had set me up.

An hour after I met Chiampa, a car drove by Charlie Brown's store. A shotgun came out the window of the car and aimed at the store window. The cash register was just inside the window and Charlie usually stood there with his back to the street. Three shotgun deer slugs crashed through the store window and hit the register. One slug splintered and ricocheted into a customer's arm. Charlie wasn't there but he got the message. He went into hiding for two weeks. Meanwhile, I traced that white car through its license plate number to a car rental agency that Sammy Linden owned. Sammy was with the McLaughlins and the Hughes brothers.

A police car started parking near my apartment. I knew the cop in the car and I knew what punk he was related to.

I was still looking for Charlie Brown when Buddy McLean asked me to let it slide. He said Freddy Hicky asked him to call it off. Hicky ran a bar on Summer Street in East Boston and came up with a lot of information on the enemy. It was important to the war to keep him happy.

"Okay," I said, "but I'll get that weasel later."

I didn't. Charlie Brown came out of hiding and was so happy to be alive he started giving us vital information. And the police car stopped parking near my apartment.

2

I met Bobbi up at the West End Club run by Peter Limone. The club was on Cambridge Street near the Charles Street Jail. Everyone who was anyone turned up at the Club sooner or later. On this particular night when I walked in with Chico and Nicky, the Bear was there. I was having a drink with the Bear when this broad came along. The Bear said she was his girlfriend and put his arm around her.

Bobbi was a hair stylist who worked in Brookline. She had an Italian's olive skin and enough womanly assets so she never had to feel cheated. We talked for awhile and I left.

About a week later at the Surf Club in Revere she walked in. We got to talking and I bought her a drink. Chico and Nicky always sat some distance away from me to keep an eye on people. When Bobbi told me she wasn't the Bear's girl, just his friend, I asked her to meet me at the Ebbtide the next night. She did, and later I took her to Swartzie's place where the show crowd goes to eat after the joints close.

Well, I started seeing Bobbi regularly and we ended up in a few motels. One night in the summer we agreed to take a blanket, a bottle of Lancer's wine and some weed and go to the East Boston Park. It's an area near Logan Airport which is used for picnicking. Has hills and trees and grass on the edge of the water, and is pretty and private.

We drove into the park through a back entrance I knew about and walked a hundred yards or so from the car to a couple of trees on the grassy hillside. Like almost all girls from the North End, Bobbi was a sharp dresser, but she looked even better without clothes. So after getting it on awhile, we were relaxing on the blanket naked while we smoked weed and drank wine. The atmosphere was terrific. We could see planes landing and taking off, and all the airport lights. It was a warm and beautiful summer evening, the peaceful loneliness and each other.

I noticed this car pull in but I didn't pay no attention until all of a sudden I heard gunfire and the sound of people screaming or whooping. Then the car went speeding off. By then I was behind a tree with a gun in my hand and Bobbi beside me. No respectable gangster wants to be caught with his drawers off, and instantly I was thinking Bobbi had set me up. But then I realized it was just a bunch of kids shooting a gun for the fun of it.

Bobbi knew who I was, of course, and that I was in the gang war, so she understood. But even so, the mood was spoiled. We got out of there and never went back again.

Now that I look back on it, I can see it was rather funny but at the time it wasn't.

3

Word came by phone that Stevie Flemmi, also known as "the Rifleman" and the Bear's brother, wanted to see me urgently at Walter's Bar in Dorchester. Nicky and Chico went with me, of course. When we drove up Stevie was waiting. He jumped in the back seat and we drove on a couple of miles and parked.

Stevie said: "This is red hot. The law has a bug on Jerry Anguilo's phone—and so do we. I listened to the tapes myself. I heard Jerry say he was going to have you killed no matter what it cost. Also, we found out that Jerry met with the Hughes brothers down in Haymarket Square."

I said: "What else did you hear?"

"Joe," said Stevie, "everything points to the fact he is paying to have you killed. I got in touch with you as quick as I could."

I thanked Stevie, pumped him hard, and then I set up a meet with Henry Tameleo at the Tiger Tail Lounge—another joint owned by Anguilo. When I walked in Henry was sitting at a back table with some people. He excused himself and we went further back to a lone table. I said: "Henry, there isn't a thing I've done since I met you that I didn't get yours and Raymond's approval first."

Henry said: "That's right."

I said: "I can't help the heat I get from the law. People are trying to kill me and until these people are gone or don't want to kill me no more, I have no choice but to say 'Fuck the law.' I'd rather have the heat and be alive than have no heat and be dead."

My eyes had started to water. I was hurt and angry because I knew this man, and Raymond, *had* to know what Anguilo was plotting. I said: "Don't mistake these tears in my eyes for fear because they're not."

Henry said: "Calm down and tell me what's bothering you."

I said: "Jerry Anguilo is plotting to kill me."

Henry asked: "Where did you hear this?"

"Friends of mine got it from the law and from tapes of a bugged phone conversation they heard themselves."

"Did you hear the tapes, Joe?" I said: "No, but these guys are my friends and don't play games with me."

Henry said: "Jerry couldn't plan a hit without Raymond's say so, and if Raymond knows it then I'd know it. The rule is that Raymond has to okay every hit. If Jerry does a hit without Raymond's okay, Jerry dies. I'm telling you this is all wrong information you've got. If Raymond ever wanted you out of the way I'd use four favors Raymond owes me to stop a move on you, Joe."

"Henry," I said. "Everybody in this city knows I look up to you more than any man living. I told Raymond to his face I like you more than him because I've spent days with you and only hours with him."

Henry said: "Raymond respected you more for saying it than he does those other ass-kissers."

"What am I going to do?" I asked. "I don't want to upset no applecart but I can't let Jerry send somebody after me."

"You don't do nothing," Henry said. "I'll speak to Raymond tomorrow and we'll track all this down."

I said: "Okay."

Henry said: "I'll be glad when this war is over. You should have taken the jobs Raymond and I offered you in Vegas to get you out of this."

Well, I didn't disbelieve Henry exactly, but that night I called Buddy McLean and some others and they spread the word to meet at 10 A.M. next day at Buddy's place. We went into a private room. There were, roughly, some thirty people present representing seventy-five men, all capable and proven. The Bear wasn't there—he was in hiding at that particular time. After everybody was talked out, Buddy said: "I want everybody here to know that I'm sending word to

Raymond that Joe is my partner. If anybody tries to kill him, I'll try with my life to stop it, and if he dies I'll avenge his death."

Ordinary people may find this statement sick, but I considered it a statement by a man among men, a man who valued human friendship more than life itself.

All those present agreed with Buddy and the message was put on paper with seventy-five names under it. Buddy wanted to know who we could get to deliver the warning and I nominated Ronnie Casesso. It was a mistake.

A day or two later Buddy called me up to his corner. He said: "Listen to this. I just went out to see Raymond. He told me that Ronnie delivered the message and said you said we didn't trust him because he's an Italian like Raymond."

"What!" I said. "Forget it," said Buddy. "I've straightened it out, but you tell Casesso if he ever comes up here again I'll blow his head off."

I called Henry and Henry said: "Ronnie told me about the Italian bit and I was the one who told Raymond. About eight hours later Ronnie called up and told me not to tell Raymond."

Later I got hold of Ronnie. I said: "You had to play Office politics, but you're the one who's suffering. Buddy said don't you go near his place or he'll blow your head off. Ronnie, you're a piece of shit."

Raymond was more than glad to stop anything Jerry was planning for me. He didn't want seventy-five cuckoos running around loose. He didn't have any strength like that. Of course he might have been able to reach out to New York and Detroit and Florida, but, no, Raymond didn't want to tangle with Buddy McLean in any shape, manner or form. Everything quieted down and my cuckoo, the Bear, came out of hiding and when his brother told him what had happened the Bear called Larry Biaoni and said: "Listen, only two people mean anything to me and they are Stevie and Joe Barboza. I feel to blame for Joe being in this war and whatever happens to him I'll avenge."

Biaoni was bold enough to say: "There's too many of us for you, Jimmy."

The Bear replied: "Yeah, Larry, but I promise you this—before I get it nine of you will be dead and you might be in the bunch."

It was brave talk and I appreciated it. Matter of fact, I felt the same way about him.

Shortly after that, sometime in June, 1965, I called the Bear from the Ebbtide at 9:45 P.M. and agreed to meet him at Dearborn Square in an hour. When I got there Peter Paulos ran up and said: "There's been some trouble at the Bear's house."

I called his house. The babysitter was crying. "He's been shot," she said.

I ran out to the car. Just then Wimpy Bennett and Stevie came around the corner and a detective car pulled up. Two detectives got out and one said: "He's at City Hospital."

We all piled into cars and raced to City Hospital. When we got there a detective said: "He isn't bad." I sighed with relief. We waited about an hour and a doctor came down and said: "We don't know if he's going to live."

"What?" I screamed.

I went insane, kicking the wall, screeching obscenities. People who tried to calm me, I shoved aside. The law decided to get us off the street for a cooling-off period. The police rounded us all up and took us down to headquarters. A couple of hours passed and Stevie got word that his brother was going to live. An hour later the cops brought in Connie Hughes and he was visibly shaken. I told Wimpy: "I'm going to knock him off right here."

Wimpy said: "No, Connie wasn't involved because I called his house ten minutes after it happened and he was there. But I'll bet his brother (Stevie Hughes) was involved."

I went over to Connie and said: "Jimmy (the Bear) is going to live. I've an idea who was involved and I'm going to kill him."

He said: "I don't blame you, Joe; it was a bad thing."

The police let us go after holding us six hours. They were careful to escort Connie out and see him away safely. Later I found out what happened to the Bear. After talking to me on the phone, he came outside with his hands in his side pockets, one on a gun. He spotted three men. As they raised their arms he saw two shotguns and a pistol. It was Stevie Hughes and Punchie McLaughlin with the shotguns and Jim O'Toole with the pistol. They fired at him. The blast flipped him backward and he turned over completely in the air and landed on his feet with his gun in his hand. He fired as they ran. Then he fell over with eight double-ought slugs in his stomach, chest and side, and also two .38 slugs.

They had tubes running out of his lungs. The doctor said he needed a wire net inside his stomach to hold his guts in. His chest had scars going every which way. But when I finally got to see him a week later he was arguing with his brother about Peter Paulos who owed him some money. I said: "You're all right, you bald-headed fuck, when you can start worrying about money."

4

I had a plan all laid out to get Connie and Stevie Hughes. For seven nights in a row we waited in the bushes near Connie's house and neither one of them showed. Then I got into trouble with the cops outside the Ebbtide. Guy Frizzi caused it and when the beef started he left Chico and me hassling with the law and ran off. I was kept in the Charles Street Jail until Attorney F. Lee Bailey got the bail lowered. Statopoulos the Greek was in the next cell and he wouldn't come out, but I talked with him a lot and heard a lot of stories. He told me that Connie Hughes got a veteran's check the first of every month. So when I got out of jail I told Chico to go by the North Shore Shopping Center bank and see if he could spot Connie or his car. I figured Connie would cash the check as soon as he got it and one was due.

Chico left with Guy Frizzi. They came back about ninety minutes later and told me they almost got Connie. Then Guy left and Chico told me what really happened.

When they got to the bank, there was Connie coming out. Chico jumped out of the car and put a rag on Guy's rear license plate to conceal it. Guy said: "What are you doing?"

Chico said: "I'm going to shoot him."

Guy said: "No. Wait till he leaves."

Chico said: "Look, there he is eighty yards away and nobody within fifty feet of him."

Guy said: "Wait until he's on the highway and I'll pull up close and you can shoot him then."

"Okay," said Chico.

Connie drove out of the parking lot and they followed. He took the ramp on the expressway to the Mystic Bridge. Chico was slouched in the rear seat of Guy's car with the M-1 rifle ready and the back window open. He kept telling Guy to pull up closer and Guy kept stalling. Then, suddenly, Connie took the Chelsea exit. They followed and Connie noticed them for the first time. He sped across the center aisle when he got to the bottom of the ramp and shot up another ramp back to the expressway. When he was almost at the top Chico fired a quick shot and blew the window out the back. Connie didn't get hit and Guy sped away as fast as he could.

It was a day of narrow escapes for Connie Hughes. That night I was in an alley with a carbine in my hand when this guy came walking along. I said: "You'll leave with more than you came if you don't leave now, mister."

He turned around and headed back down Havre Street and suddenly I realized it was Connie. I got Chico and Patsy

Fabiano and put them in one car to go look and I got in a car with a friend of mine named Sid. By then we could see Connie getting into a car and backing down the one-way street. He was facing the right way but moving the wrong way.

We cut down Brooks Street, took a right on to Chelsea. Just before we got to Marion we spotted Connie's car coming out. Behind the wheel was Maxie Shackelford. Next to him was Connie and in the back seat was Stevie Hughes.

I pointed my rifle out the window and I jacked a shell into the chamber, but in my haste the gun jammed. Bullets were flying all around us. I said: "Pass them while I clear this gun."

Sid drove by them but by the time I cleared the gun, they had stopped and backed up again onto Marion Street and turned down a side street by a school. Then they disappeared.

Chico and Fabiano lost them too.

Sid's car had a crack in the windshield from a bullet. In the center of the door on the passenger side was a bullet hole. The bullet had gone through the door and lodged in the armrest. If it hadn't been for the armrest I'd got it in the side. Guess it was fired as we went by them.

Next day Guy Frizzi showed up and I asked him where he had gone the night before. He said he was with Ginny. Now Ginny was a 15-year-old girl that Guy was feeding goofballs to and going to bed with.

Guy said: "I slapped Ginny last night and broke up with her."

I said: "Fuck Ginny. Do you know what happened last night?"

"No," said Guy.

I told him and Guy said: "I'm going to leave the state for awhile."

I said: "It figures. I got people shooting at me and you're going to leave me here to face it by myself. Do me a favor and go."

Later on we heard that one of the bullets fired during the
chase went into a house, entered the parlor and just missed a
woman's head who was sitting there watching TV. There was
an old gangster movie on that night and I wondered if she'd
been looking at it.

About 3 P.M. the day Guy left, Ginny came over. She was
a cute little thing but, God, so young. She asked for Guy and
I told her he had left on vacation. So then she said: "Will you
give him this?"

She handed me a little box. I opened it. Inside was a .22
bullet, a .32 and a .38 bullet, a .45 and a .357 bullet, and some
shotgun slugs.

I said: "What are you doing with this, Ginny?"

She said: "Guy gave them to me from his guns. I saved
them for mementos, but Guy and I have broke up and I don't
want to bother with them any more. He's a mean son of a
bitch."

I said: "I could tell you a lot of things he is."

She said: "You'd be surprised at what I could tell you,
Joe."

I said: "You'll have to do a lot of growing up first, Ginny."

She said: "Oh, yeah. Supposing I tell you I know about
the shooting yesterday."

"What shooting, Ginny?"

She said: "Guy told me that Chico could have killed
Connie Hughes yesterday if he had fired continuously but
that he was nervous and only fired once. Guy said he should
have done it himself and it would've been done right."

"What else did he tell you?" I asked.

"He told me all about the gang war and how nothing is
done without him there to do it."

I stared at this child with all this information. Then I
said: "Guy is just yapping to look big. He and nobody else
around here are involved in anything."

She said: "Don't lie to me, Joe Barboza."

I said: "Go to school and blow your nose while you're at it."

She said: "Guy don't treat me young. He says I'm sweet meat when he goes down on me."

I said: "Guy isn't around here and won't be for awhile, so don't you come or you'll get your little butt slapped."

She said: "Joe, go and fuck yourself." Then she stomped away.

Guy came back two weeks later. I didn't say anything to him. What was the use? Besides, I had a trial coming up. Then one day Guy said to me: "Look, why don't I let Freddie Chiampa buy my end of the shylock business? He wants to be partners with you bad. Once he gives me the money, we'll whack him out and cut up the bread."

I said: "He already happens to be a partner of mine and a damn good one. He doesn't shoot off his mouth to little kids about how tough he is."

Guy said: "Whatta you mean?"

I said: "Here are the bullets you gave Ginny. She told me a lot."

"What did she say?" snarled Guy.

I said: "Find out for yourself."

Guy said: "I'll break her fucking head."

I said: "You ought to look good doing it because that's about your speed."

5

Some people thought Punchie McLaughlin led a charmed life. I didn't think so and neither did Buddy McLean. Any way you looked at it though, it had been a violent one.

Back in the fifties, Punchie had a fight with Rocky Sullivan. It was a good match since both men were ex-pros. But Rocky had been a main event fighter. What's more Rocky worked as a longshoreman and kept in good condition while

Punchie was a slob. The trouble started with an argument. Then Punchie hit Rocky from behind with an iron pipe, knocking Rocky to the floor. Punchie swung again, but Rocky rolled out of the way and got to his feet with blood pouring down his face. One of his punches tore Punchie's ear. The fight carried them outside where Punchie finally wilted and rolled under a car to get away. To the amazement of the watching people, Rocky lifted up one end of the car and put a wheel on the sidewalk. That gave him enough room to go under the car after Punchie who was hollering: "No more, no more."

Punchie waited years for revenge but he finally had Harold Hannon call Rocky over to a car one day. Hannon shot Rocky dead.

After the gang war started, Punchie and a man named Earle drove up to a spot near Boston Commons. Earle stayed with the car while Punchie went somewhere, but when Punchie came back, Earle was gone. Punchie was sitting there waiting when a gunman let loose with a shotgun on the driver's side of the car. The blast hit Punchie on the lower jaw. He tried to get out the passenger side when another shotgun blast hit the other side of his face. Punchie lay there all bloody with his jaw hanging open. The gunman thought he was dead and left. After a lot of surgery, Punchie recovered.

Months later Punchie was driving down the street near the expressway in Dedham. A car with Buddy McLean inside opened fire with a M-1 rifle. A bullet hit Punchie inside the wrist and exited through the outside of the hand. Punchie drove up the wrong way on an exit ramp and got away, but his right hand had to be amputated.

His brother Georgie went to see him in the hospital and Punchie said: "All this because you had to be a wise guy."

It was right after this shooting that police caught Georgie McLaughlin hiding out from a warrant charging him with murdering a young bankteller at a Roxbury party. Georgie was drunk and had a quarrel with a guy. He left and waited outside. The bankteller looked like the guy Georgie was sore at, so when he came out Georgie shot him down by mistake. The cops put Georgie in the old Charles Street Jail, an ancient structure next door to the Massachusetts General Hospital.

The exercise yard faced Cambridge Street and was surrounded by apartment buildings with clotheslines on their flat roofs. From those roofs you could look right down into the exercise yard. Ronnie and I climbed up there one day for a look. It was beautiful, roughly a 75-yard shot.

After thinking about it we decided it'd be safer to shoot from a window in an apartment. Less chance of being seen. Ronnie had it figured we could get in there an hour before Georgie got his exercise. If nobody was home we'd open the lock with a strip of celluloid. If somebody was home we'd tie them up. I figured on three rifles just to be sure. We'd get everybody in and out by dressing them as house painters and stealing a painter's truck for them to drive.

There was only one problem. Georgie was on a paranoid trip because of some of the people in jail with him, and he wouldn't leave his cell. Then we got word he was exercising all by himself in a small yard between the guard room and the woman's section on the hospital side of the jail. I went over to the side street which separated the jail and the hospital and went into a side entrance. On the third floor of the hospital I found a window looking right down into Georgie's private yard. It was even better—only a 50-yard shot.

I drove over to Ronnie's place and told him to get me an oil filter from a diesel truck. Ronnie asked why. I said: "Because it's a perfect silencer for a rifle. I can't be blasting inside a hospital and have everybody come running."

But all this preparation was in vain. Georgie's trial started and we shifted targets. It figured that Punchie would be going to the trial to give his brother moral support. If he didn't he'd lose face. Besides, we figured the law would take care of Georgie. If it didn't we'd try again later, but, meanwhile it was Punchie who needed personal attention.

One day in October, 1965, Punchie started to the courthouse for the trial. Since he couldn't drive himself, having only one hand left, and nobody wanted to drive him, he planned to take the bus. I guess it seemed safe—broad daylight, a lot of eyewitnesses, heavy traffic. He was standing at the bus stop with about six people when a gold-colored car pulled up. A man was driving and there was another man in the back seat with a handgun. At the same time across the street, a four-door Chevy pulled up. It was the crash car, intended to delay any pursuit of the hitman's getaway car, if necessary. A passenger got out and stood directly on the corner opposite Punchie's corner. His job was to back up the hit man and get Punchie if anything went wrong. He would then have jumped into the gold-colored car to escape.

The hit man wore a wig resembling a crew cut hair style, and horn-rimmed glasses with plain glass. He was supposed to wear a mustache, but didn't. He walked up to Punchie and shot him five times. The last bullet went through his scrotum. Punchie was holding a paper bag with his gun inside. Apparently his last conscious thought was the realization he would be searched by police. He handed the bag to a woman and then fell over dead.

Three hours after the shooting I was picked up down at my corner. My gold-colored car was found in front of Patsy Fabiano's house. A squad of police checked it out. They found a suitcase in the car with some wigs, makeup and the like. I told them some show business broad left it in my car. They held me for eleven hours and had some women witnesses try to identify me through a one-way glass window. I knew they were there and I kept screaming: "You'd better be fucking sure." Well, they weren't sure, and eventually the police let me go.

Connie and Stevie Hughes were the main ones left. Once

we had them the gang war would be over. Georgie was out of it. The jury had found him guilty of first degree murder and he was on Death Row. Things were shaping up at last.

6

It was the latter part of October. About 8 P.M. I pulled up at my corner. Blu Di'Agostino and Ricco Sacramoth came out of the coffee shop and said they were on their way to Winter Hill to see Buddy McLean. That reminded me I wanted to call Buddy so I went into Benbrook Drugstore and phoned him.

"Hello," said the voice at the Tap Royal.

I said: "Tell Buddy the Seagull is calling." ("Seagull" was the code word Buddy and I used when calling each other.)

Buddy came to the phone and we exchanged insults. I told him I was running down some good information on the Fat Guy, meaning Stevie Hughes. He said: "I wish you'd come up, you ugly Portugee. I miss you."

"If I come up I'll take that pretty Portugee nurse away from you," I said.

"That'll be the day, Seagull," he said.

"Listen," I said, "Ricco and Blu are on their way up there now."

"That's good," said Buddy.

I said: "Well, I'm going to leave you now. Take care, Seagull."

"Be careful and keep your right hand high, Seagull," Buddy said.

I hung up and went outside. Chico, Nicky and I drove off. Hours went by. It was 3 A.M. and I was up at the West End Club on Cambridge Street. It was Peter Limone's afterhours joint and the place was loaded with people. Peter came over to me.

"How are you, Joe?" said Peter.

"All right, Peter," I said. "Give me fifteen hundred at one percent if you can."

"Okay, Joe. Got another good juice loan?"

"Yeah," I said. "One hundred and fifty a week minus the fifteen weekly I'll have to give to you. One thirty-five is good. Don't you think so, Peter?"

"Can't beat that," said Peter. "Here, here's your money."

He slapped me on my back and left. I said to Chico: "I can't stand that two-faced bastard. He hates my guts but doesn't have the balls to say so."

Sonny Mecurio walked over. Sonny said: "Hey, did you hear the news? Buddy McLean got shot tonight." I smiled. "You're wrong, Sonny. I was just talking to Buddy tonight."

Sonny said: "Joe, he got shot about midnight. Blu Di'Agostino and Ricco Sacramoni got shot too."

I froze. It had to be true when he mentioned Blu and Ricco. Finally I asked: "What happened?"

Sonny said: "The news reported it happened in Winter Hill. They're all alive but Buddy is in bad condition."

I stomped out of the club and found out what I wanted to know.

Roughly about midnight, Buddy had come walking out of a pizza parlor about seven stores down from the Tap Royal. Blu and Ricco were with him. They went back toward the Tap Royal. Right next to it was an abandoned theater. The marquee was still there but the ribwork was showing. Stevie Hughes was there inside the building. He saw Buddy, Blu and Ricco. Buddy had $3,500 in his pocket, his share of $13,000 Henry Tameleo had paid for a truck load of cigarettes.

Buddy had opened the door of his car parked in front of the Tap Royal and was behind the door when Stevie let loose with a shotgun. Buddy wasn't hurt but Ricco and Blu went down. Buddy stepped out, grabbed them, and was pulling them behind the car when Stevie fired again. The shot hit Buddy in the head. He fell. Stevie ran out the back of the theater and got into a waiting car which had his brother Connie at the wheel. They got hold of their girlfriends and such men as they had, left and got drunk to celebrate.

Buddy died a few hours later. If he had lived he'd been a vegetable. At his funeral were politicians, union officials and attorneys. Everybody couldn't get into the church, there were so many people.

I was at the wake in the afternoon. The coffin was closed. I spoke to Howie Winters and Tommy Ballou. When I left I walked by four detectives who were observing the crowd. One of them asked me: "Hey, Joe, who's in there?"

"A lot of people I don't know," I said.

The detectives arrested Tommy Ballou on a warrant for something. Ricco and Blu went back to prison as parole violators. They recovered from their wounds but Blu's arm was never the same again.

A man was dead. But he had lived to see Bernie and Punchie dead and Georgie in Death Row. The war would go on without him.

7

Raymond Distasio lived in Medford in a white house behind a school. He was on the McLaughlin–Hughes side in the gang war and had helped Punchie hunt for Buddy McLean back in the summer before Buddy and Punchie were killed. That was enough to make him hot, but then he borrowed $15,000 from the Office and couldn't meet his payments. When the sharks tried to hassle him he told them they would get their money when he had it. And that made him hotter.

About a month after Buddy died, three men went down to Distasio's house one morning to shoot him from the school yard as he stepped into his car. But he had already left and was on his way to the Mickey Mouse Lounge where he had a shylock business for the construction workers who were building apartments in the area.

That evening at almost 5 P.M. on the nose, a car pulled up on the sidewalk in front of the entrance. The driver got out as did two men from the back seat. A fourth man stayed in front with a carbine in his hand. There was a fifth man nearby in a legit car which he was ready to stall in the middle of the street.

Of the three who went into the Mickey Mouse Lounge, one stopped near the door with a carbine in his hand. He wore a hood, topcoat and sunglasses. The other two walked to the front of the bar with their heads bent forward. One said: "Brrr, it's cold."

He had on a rain-and-shine coat with a hood and a soft hat to hide the hood. He wore gloves and he had one hand behind his back. It was holding a .38 pistol on a .45 frame. The other man was dressed the same way and was holding a .45 behind his back.

Distasio was in the middle of the dance floor. At the bar was John O'Neil. He lived in New Hampshire and had supplied guns to Distasio to sell to the McLaughlins. When the two gunmen lifted their heads and looked around, Distasio started running toward O'Neil. The gunman with the .38 on the .45 frame fired and Distasio fell. O'Neil became hysterical and started screaming: "I don't want to die."

The gunmen hadn't intended to kill O'Neil, but his hysteria left them no choice. When he ran away from the bar and across the dance floor, they followed. Stopping only long enough to pump a couple of more shots into the head of the fallen Distasio, they chased O'Neil all the way to a glass door before they shot him. The .38 had jammed but the gunman used a second pistol, an airweight snubnose .38.

With the job done, the two men ran outside and got into the car. They drove toward Lynn over the General Edwards Bridge. They stopped at a shopping center and threw the guns into some weeds near the Charter House Motel. At that point they also changed cars, leaving the stolen vehicle behind.

The *Boston Globe* came out with a story about the shooting. I don't remember the exact words but this is how the story started: "A man known around the city as the Animal, and one of his beasties, walked into the Mickey Mouse Lounge yesterday. The Animal shot Raymond Distasio and the beastie shot John O'Neil when O'Neil didn't move fast enough..."

"I'm going to sue the paper," I told Wimpy Bennett.

"Forget it," said Wimpy. "This is a good shot in the arm for our side. Now that Buddy is dead, people have you taking his place."

"Fuck you," I said. "I don't want to take nobody's place."

The gang war went on and the Office kept using it to solve problems.

5

The Tightening Circle

The gang war imposed a certain discipline upon the Boston underworld which began to evaporate with the deaths of the principal leaders of the warring factions. Immediately, the Mafia tried to move into the leadership vacuum. The major obstacle to a takeover was Joe Barboza, a strong man with the nucleus of a gang of his own. Barboza was handicapped in 1966, however. For much of it he was helpless in prison and upon release was very much a marked man with both cops and killers on his trail.

1

The cops thought they had me cold. They were laughing. I was indicted for assaulting a police officer, possession of a firearm, possession of marijuana and disturbing the peace. When the cops argued that I was safer off the street, bail was set at $100,000. Attorney F. Lee Bailey appealed and got the bond reduced to $35,000, which I easily made. I came to trial in January, 1966, and was found guilty of disturbing the peace. Big deal! I got six months at Deer Island and the cops stopped laughing.

Deer Island wasn't so isolated that they couldn't bring me back to Chelsea to stand trial on a traffic charge. I was sitting there in the court all cuffed when in came those two troublemakers, Chico and Nicky. They were sporting new jackets and they looked at me as proud as peacocks. They knew I was familiar with every stitch of clothes they had and they knew I'd be curious. So those two bull mooses strutted around, rubbing their nails on their lapels and blowing air on their nails. Chico said to me: "You convict, you."

Finally Judge McLeod started in on me. I liked the judge. He used to roar from the bench and make you think he was going to hang you, but he was fair and gave a judgment on the merits of your case and not on the hate of the police officers.

My attorney, Al Farese, said: "He was speeding, your honor. He was fleeing some police officers who he thought was someone else."

Judge McLeod said: "If he lived a better life, he wouldn't be fleeing."

Farese said: "He changed his name to Baron so he can change his life."

The judge said: "Mr. Farese, when Barboza changes we'll all be living on the moon." He slapped his gavel down and said: "Thirty-five dollars fine."

I was laughing like everybody else, but suddenly I stopped laughing. The law was waiting for Chico and Nicky outside the courtroom and they were pinched for possession of stolen property—their coats.

I screamed: "Those two can't even let me do time in peace."

But my anger left me. I sent them to Harry Khaim who ran a Greek belly-dancing club. Khaim had a judge he could move. It cost me bail money and $500 for each of them, but they beat the beef.

In March or April, Wimpy Bennett managed to ambush Stevie Hughes, but Stevie was hard to kill. His spleen was removed and his kidneys damaged, but he lived. Then in May came the news that Connie Hughes had been killed.

The Boston newspapers managed to drag me into it by implication. They explained that Connie had been given a contract by a Mafia member—Larry Biaone was implied but not named—to kill a man in the Deer Island House of Correction. The man—and I was implied—allegedly sent out word to kill Connie first.

I was so happy Connie was dead I didn't care what the newspapers said about me. Pretty soon I got the details of the hit.

Connie was in a bar in Charlestown near the Mystic Bridge. John Locke, a tall, skinny pill-headed kid, was there with him. It was late at night and Connie was trying to get information about the location of Howie Winters, one of Buddy McLean's partners. The guy he was quizzing wouldn't talk. Connie stabbed him in the leg. The attempt had taken an hour, and in Charlestown that was too long. Most of the people there who knew what was going on were on the McLean side. So the grapevine got to working and in a matter of an hour there were people waiting outside the bar for Connie to come out.

Eventually Connie came out and got into his car. The men waiting in two cars followed as he drove toward the Mystic Bridge. The windows in the back doors of both cars were open and on the back seats of both cars lay a man with a rifle, unseen. The rifles were carbines with a thirty-round banana clip attached.

Connie paid his fare at the tollgate. So did the drivers of the two cars behind him. The back seat passengers sat up until they were through the gate. Connie was in the center lane now, driving slow as he always did when he was trying to see if he was being followed. One of the cars began passing him on his right and the other on his left. They edged ahead until their rear windows were even with his hood. Abruptly the men in the rear seats stuck their rifles through the windows, pointing them back at Connie. He was in a crossfire. The guns opened up. Sixty bullets riddled the car and Connie.

Buddy McLean would have been pleased to know who had half avenged him. I, of course, had an alibi. The night Connie was killed I was eating a stolen filet mignon from the warden's refrigerator. The next night, after I got the news, I lay on my bed smoking a joint of marijuana. I was happy for the gang war was almost over.

2

While I was in Deer Island, Guy Frizzi, Chico and Nicky took care of the shylock business. Chico's girl, Elaine, got a job in town as a barmaid at the Attic and Chico started hanging around there. They all became buddies with Arthur "Tashi" Bratsos, Johnny and Jimmy Marteranno and Tommy DiPrisco. So when I got out of jail they took me down and introduced me and we hit it off good. I started using the Attic as a base for my shylocking business. About twenty-five people a night came to see me on business so I kept the joint packed. Occasionally we'd go over to the Sahara Club in the South End. Tashi had an interest in it. The Sahara was a big place with booths along the wall and a big dance floor in the center.

One night the law came in while I was there. The place had about 150 people in it, including 20 hookers. They asked everybody for their identification but they don't say nothing to me. Finally, after a half hour, they came over. One of them said: "All right, Barboza, let's go."

I said: "For what?"

He said: "We found a gun in the closet of the office."

I said: "I'm sitting sixty feet from that office. I've never even been in that office. Yeah, I'd better go, you motherfucker, before you find some insane excuse to shoot me."

They started leading me out and Chico said: "Joe, where you going?"

I said: "To my second home."

As they put me in the car, Chico screamed: "You can't leave him alone, can you? You won't be satisfied until they find some of you on the street with your heads blown off."

They drove me to Station Four. In behind me they brought Howie Winters in handcuffs. Howie is normally a quiet, soft-spoken guy, but he was bug-eyed with anger and cursing and screaming. I was dumbfounded but I didn't need to say anything since Howie had said it all and more.

The cops told the station cops what Chico had said and they went back in swarms to get him. He ran out the back door and got away but not before he sprained his ankle real bad.

Howie and I spent the night at the station. I didn't catch crabs this time. We were taken to court and were waiting in the tank for our case to be called when Attorney Farese came to the window. I said: "I want to sue these people."

He said: "Sign this paper promising you won't sue and they'll let you and Howie go."

"They have all the answers, don't they?"

Farese said: "If you don't sign you'll have to pay a high bail and attorney fees."

I signed.

The law was still upset about Chico's remark and they told me all about it. When I saw Chico, I said: "You and your big mouth," and I slapped him on his sprained ankle. He let out a howl and then smiled.

Problems I still had. I was really uptight about Guy Frizzi. Chico and Nicky couldn't stand him and nobody else could for long. He had been going with Carlotta, a belly dancer, but he beat her often and even broke her arm. Frizzi called Nutilly's wife a nigger-fucker and shamed me in front of twenty people when he let Nutilly beat him up. I had to go after Nutilly, an old customer, with a shotgun and make him go into hiding in order to keep respect. Nutilly's wife was a nice woman but Frizzi was mad because she wouldn't go to bed with him. The Bear didn't like Frizzi and Eddie Fisher didn't want him around his office. He talked to customers like they were shit and even though I gave all the beatings they hated him worse than me. When I got out of Deer Island, Frizzi said: "Well, you've had a five month vacation; now it's my turn." He left with his family for California and I decided I'd buy him out when he got back.

Meanwhile, Chico stabbed Arthur Pearson outside the Tiger Tail Lounge. Nicky and I were present. The law picked me up and I was put on high bail, but the law couldn't get an indictment because Pearson wouldn't testify. Maybe the $10,000 I gave his father with a promise of $10,000 more when the case was over helped some. There was another witness, a girl. I had Tony C from Everett make a play for the girl and gave him $100 a week to take her out and romance her. They got engaged and I had to get Tony a one carat diamond ring. The plan was he would marry her, if necessary, all the while persuading her not to testify. When the case was dropped he'd get a divorce. The whole case was sticky and I was sore at Chico because I never wanted him to stab Pearson in the first place.

While Frizzi was still in California, Carlotta, the belly dancer, came up to me in the Normandy where she was dancing. She said: "For months Guy has been telling me you were going to kill me. Guy knocks you continually. He says it should be him going to Rhode Island to see Patriarca, not you. He gives me beatings, never gives me money, but don't want me to work."

She told a lot more and ended by saying: "I'm telling you this because he's everything you're not, a phony, two-faced coward."

Guy came back from California and I said: "I'm buying you out." Tashi bought his end for $15,000 and the promise of $30,000 more in two weeks. We had about $50,000 working on the street and it was bringing in $5,000 a week vig. Guy didn't want to sell and he went around to all our customers and tried to persuade them to stay with him. They wouldn't have anything to do with him. After that he hated me and tried to double-cross me. Now he's scared and that's the only reason he's alive today. I'd rather he run frightened; death is too good for him.

3

I wasn't the only one having troubles. A gang of cowboys was sticking up a lot of Office connected card games and the like. The Office was upset about it and even blamed me. Claimed one of the stick-up men looked like Chico. I had to protest to Jerry Anguilo and warn him I wouldn't stand for such shit.

About 10 P.M. one day I was sitting in Chiambi's Bar, a few doors down from the corner of Bennington and Brooks. In walked Benny, Mario and the Pig. They told me they were going on a score and were waiting for Rocco DeSeglio to pick them up. When he showed up in his maroon-colored T-bird, Benny got in and drove, the Pig sat in the back, and Mario sat on the passenger side of the front seat. That left DeSeglio sitting in the middle between the bucket seats. I figured he'd be uncomfortable but Mario said it wouldn't be for long. They drove off.

About 11 A.M. next day, I was back in Chiambi's Bar taking care of business. Benny came in and asked to talk to me outside. Mario and the Pig were waiting and we went across the street and stood on the sidewalk next to Barney's. Benny said: "We killed Rocco DeSeglio and left him in Danvers Woods."

"They haven't found him yet," said Mario. "We weren't going on a score like we told you last night; we were setting him up."

"Why?" I said.

"Jerry made us do it," said Benny.

Eventually, I got the story out of them.

Rocco was a professional fighter, a welterweight and a slugger type. I had met him while training and he'd been a customer of mine. It was Rocco, Benny, Mario and the Pig who had been sticking up the Office barbut games and the card games. Jerry found out that DeSeglio was the inside man who saw to it the door was unlocked for the others to come in. Once he had that figured, it wasn't hard to trace out who Rocco traveled with and they fit the description of the gunmen.

Jerry called them all in except Rocco and conned them into admitting it. They claimed, of course, they didn't know the games they were robbing were Office connected. Jerry told them he wanted Rocco taken care of. "It's either you or him," they said they were told. So they decided it would be him.

They drove out to a dark street and Mario got out as if he was going to get the hot car they were to use in making the score. That put Rocco in the bucket seat. The Pig, sitting in back, shot him. Benny added: "We drove him out of East Boston so you wouldn't get no heat."

"Thanks," I said. "Remind me never to let you guys sit in the back seat."

They put their heads down and looked away.

Later that day I called Detective Bobby Fawcett at his home. Fawcett was a tough Irish cop who was always bothering me. I told him: "I don't care if you recognize this voice or not because you'll never prove it. I want to give you a break and make you look good. If you look in the Danvers wooded area you'll find something in a car."

They found the car later that night and the Boston papers had big headlines. Fawcett came around to my corner next day and said: "Nothing has changed between you and I."

I said: "I don't know what you're talking about."

Later on I went to see Jerry at the Dog House in the North End. I told him that Benny and his friends told me why they shot Rocco.

Jerry said: "It was better to use them to solve the problem than to use Office workers."

I said: "Yeah."

4

I met Carl Villeca in Walpole in 1962. His nickname was "Bluejay" and he had a blue jay's slanting forehead and nose. His face was all pox marks, he wore glasses and he could talk the brass balls off a pawnshop. Carl wasn't a violent man but with his looks and acting ability he could make you think otherwise. When he got out of Walpole he drifted out to Lawrence, working as a car salesman, and he came up with a scheme to take over the town.

Carl started by having a friend throw a bomb outside a bar. The blast shattered windows and put fear into the hearts of some citizens. He started to move in on the bookmakers and to shake down the businessmen. For a show of strength he had Rudy Sciarre from Rhode Island come down with three other guys and meet him at the Holiday Inn where he hung out. He called me and asked me to do the same.

I came up with eight men in three Cadillacs. We parked right at the entrance of the Holiday Inn and we walked into the lounge together. People saw us clear and also saw Carl come over to shake hands. Carl was elated and said: "Everybody in the know in Lawrence will hear about this. Wow, what a show of strength!"

We went over to the bar. I said: "Carl, this isn't a show. It's for real. I'm interested in getting protection money from the lounges and nightclubs in this area."

He said: "The valley is yours. They have some good joints down there."

As it turned out, I never saw the valley, but at the time I was serious about moving in. Recently I had gone into the protection business in a big way. The Blue Bunny in Nantasket and the Louis Room at the Beach Plaza in Revere was giving me $100 a week for protection. The biggest money-maker was the Diplomat Hotel and Lounge around the corner from Police Station #4.

Fifteen hookers worked openly out of the Diplomat Lounge. The girls would sit along the wall or at the bar and the John would look them over and pick out the one he wanted. They'd go from the lounge into the hotel and up to a room. When they were through they'd come back the same way. It was convenient not having to go out of doors—especially in the winter. In one hour I watched a girl leave with three tricks. The Bear had a girl working there at one time and she averaged $800 to $1,000 a week.

I never owned a girl but I wasn't above shaking down a Mr. Pimp for his earnings. I went into it with Tashi Bratsos, and soon we had fifteen pimps paying us $100 a week. Then Tashi reported that other pimps were willing to pay $150 for the privilege of letting their "cows" graze in the Diplomat so we raised the prices and were getting $2,500 a week. But I felt dirty about it even though I refused to talk to the girls or the pimps. Yet the money meant a lot of the guys in our gang would eat better.

We were working on the joint now known as Father's Mustache. I had given the punk who ran it a month to come across and then I was going to bomb it as an example to others. Meanwhile, we were having a hassle with the Living Room, formerly the Peppermint Lounge. Peter Fumari ran it and he thought he was a wise guy. When he turned us down, some of the boys went in and tore the place up. Fumari made a deal with a hood from Cleveland who had connections out there with the Mob. This hood went to Henry Tameleo and was told to mind his own business and leave us alone. Later

Henry told me that Fumari wanted to talk shop. I told him my terms were $250 a week or $10,000 in a lump sum, and a piece of Fumari's shylock business.

Later, after I had gone back to jail, Chico told me that Fumari had forked over the money and would talk about splitting the shylock with me when I got back out.

Anyway, with all this going for me it looked fairly simple to expand out to Lawrence. Carl Villeca was willing and we made our plans. The guys in the three Caddies took me home and then they went out on the town. Next morning Tashi had a story for me.

It seems that one of our boys, Tommy DiPrisco, had a girlfriend who was a hooker. Tommy had picked her up last night after leaving me. Some Puerto Rican cat made a pass at her. Tommy got mad, left his girlfriend somewhere and went looking for the Puerto Rican. He thought he spotted him near the Prudential Center and he shot him dead.

I said: "Tashi, why the hell is he mad because some dude makes a pass at his hooker girlfriend who was being fucked all night by seventeen different guys?"

Tashi didn't know. I said: "I know. He's been dying to put his first notch on his gun and he's been looking for any excuse to do it. He's a sick one."

"Joe," said Tashi. "The guy he came back and shot wasn't the Puerto Rican who made the pass in the first place. He shot the wrong guy."

5

Back in 1965 I decided to kill Sammy Linden because I thought it'd help the Bear recover from his wounds. Before he was shot we'd been over to Providence to see Raymond Patriarca. He had told me he wanted a bookmaker roughed up and he had given the Bear a contract on Linden. The Bear was shot before he could execute it so I told Chico that killing

Linden would help the Bear more than all that new blood they were pumping into him.

Ronnie thought it was a good idea but he told me to wait until he'd checked with Raymond. I promised. But meanwhile I called Sammy and asked him to come by my corner at 2 P.M. I had the hit all figured.

Sammy was an ex-con and ex-fighter. He was small, only about five feet, five, with a round face and gray hair, and he was the best abortionist around. The cheapest you got an abortion from Sammy was $450. But even the best fail now and then, and on one occasion Sammy's patient was found floating in the Charles River.

In addition to abortions, Sammy had a numbers racket going in seven cities and twenty towns in Massachusetts. He had so much cash coming in he loaned money to the Office and to people in the Office. Once Frank Smith brought Lincoln Rockwell, the nutty Nazi cult leader to see Sammy and talked him into giving Rockwell a thousand bucks. He was friendly with the Hughes faction and gave them money. Working under Sammy were such shylocks as Johnny Gagliard and Vinnie Teresa.

Now Sammy had a big house facing the beach in Revere. It had caught fire and the windows were boarded up. My idea was to have him take me to the house and show me the fire damage. The driveway went down a ramp to the rear of the house. Nobody would see us go in—or me come out alone.

Sammy showed up for his appointment with his two little dogs, and we talked awhile. I told him I was interested in seeing his house and he agreed to take me just as soon as the phone call I was expecting came in.

Chico called me to the phone. I was very somber, having worked myself up to the point of killing Sammy.

"Hello," I said.

"Forget it," said Ronnie, "and absolutely. Don't do anything. I'll explain when I get back."

"Okay," I said.

Hanging up, I was suddenly exhausted. My body had been racing. Now everything stopped and it left me very tired.

I said: "Sammy, I have to leave right now because of that call. I'll see you later, buddy."

"Sure," said Sammy.

That night Ronnie told me that Raymond wasn't ready to have Sammy hit. He didn't know why.

All that had happened a year ago. Since then I'd been to jail and got out. The Bear had recovered and was back in prison for shooting a kid who wanted to fight him. And I was out on bail after the law had found two guns, nine joints of marijuana and Chico and me in Patsy Fabiano's car.

Sammy was still around and trying to act as a peacemaker for Stevie Hughes. He told me Stevie wanted peace. I said: "Tell him to go fuck his mother." Suddenly a pattern developed. First one guy and then another reported seeing Stevie in Revere near Sammy's house on a Friday. For some reason he was seeing Sammy on Friday. I got on the phone and talked to a lot of people. Found out that Raymond now said it was okay to hit Sammy. Turned out the reason he had waited before was to have time to borrow a lot of money from Sammy. Now that he had $80,000, it was all right to whack out Sammy. In fact, it was a good idea.

I told everybody to pass the word I was going to hide out in New York because of the Pearson case. On the next Friday people watched Sammy's house. Sure enough, Stevie Hughes showed up. A little later he got into Sammy's little blue car with Sammy and his two dogs. They were headed for Lawrence. Two cars followed them. The driver of one of the cars wore a woman's wig.

At Middletown the two cars closed in and opened fire with M-1 rifles. Sammy's fingers gripping the steering wheel were literally blown off his hands. Stevie was reaching for a gun when bullets plowed into him. The car went over an embankment. The dogs were thrown clear and were running around barking while Sammy and Stevie lay dead in the wreckage.

Buddy McLean could rest easy in his grave now— his death was completely avenged.

6

After the Hughes' shooting I was careful for two weeks and had tight security. At night when it was time to pick me up, somebody would call and say they were on their way. I'd turn on my walkie-talkie. When the three cars were outside, the guy in the lead car would give a long whistle into his walkie-talkie. If I wasn't ready I'd give a broken whistle in mine. When I was ready I'd give a long whistle, and I'd leave the house with the walkie-talkie in one hand and a .38 in the other. The three cars would be lined up. Chico in the back car would be pointing a shotgun at the closest corner of the building. Someone in the lead car would be pointing a shotgun to the other corner. The middle car would have the rear door open. I'd get in it and there would be an M-1 rifle on the floor. I'd direct the lead car by walkie-talkie where to go and the rear car would follow our direction signals.

I borrowed a lot of cars and was never found in the same car twice in one week. Meanwhile, other guys were driving my "James Bond car." The law had given it a code number-66—and they were always on the lookout for it. They stopped Dido Vacari over in New Hampshire in it and arrested him too. He had a "dangerous weapon" in the car, they said—a juggling pin.

The law started following me night and day at one point. Detectives Sullivan and Villenti followed me eight hours a day one week and state police followed me at night. They would switch the following week. One night we started out to Alphonso's. Sullivan and Villenti were behind us. I said: "You know, we say we got legal protection with these guys following us and we can always lose them if we want, but can we?"

Chico said: "Let's try."

"Okay," I said, "but we'll set them up."

We went to Alphonso's and they followed us in and sat at a separate table. I had Nick buy them a drink, and then another one. After awhile they bought one for themselves. Soon they'd had six, and I told Chico to tell them we were leaving for the Surf Club.

We went to the Surf and parked ourselves at the bar with our backs to the fire door. The detectives stood down at the end of the bar. I sent them a drink. After awhile, Villenti went to the phonebooth, closed the door and sat down hard. Sullivan got interested in the floor show and was looking away from us with one arm on the cigarette machine. I said: "Now."

Out the fire door we went and into the car laughing like kids. Off we went.

We found out what happened later because the people in the Surf had been alert that something was up and they got a laugh out of it too.

After a minute or two, Sullivan looked around and did a double take when he didn't see us. He ran to the phonebooth and rapped on the door. "They're gone," he yelled. "They're gone."

Villenti hung up the phone and they rushed out of the place but they never found us that night.

No one was following us the night John Jackson died either.

Jackson was a witness to the murder of a girl who was found on the roof of the Casa Mia Restaurant next door to the Intermission Lounge. Johnny Marteranno and Bobby Palladino were indicted for it. Word got around that Palladino as well as Jackson would testify against Johnny.

Palladino was killed first. He was in a car with two men. One of the men was in the back seat. He shot Bobby through the head. The body was dumped next to a steel girder in North Station near Boston Gardens. It was a bloody hit. The men had to throw all their clothes down a sewer and burn up the car—a Cadillac.

Jackson was hit in September, 1966. He came home about 2 A.M. When he stepped out of his car he was hit by a shotgun blast which came from behind a fence. The shotgun had been bought with phony identification from Sears.

The killer started running. Tommy DiPrisco yelled at him: "Wait, my foot is stuck."

The killer began laughing so hard he could scarcely run. DiPrisco got loose by himself.

There were no more witnesses in the Marteranno case.

7

A detective I was friendly with called me in East Boston with a tip: "Joe," he said, "the law is coming out tonight to shake you down."

I said: "What for?"

He said: "The heat's on. They want to catch you and Nicky and Chico with guns. The word is out to get you guys off the street, one way or another."

I said: "Thanks. I'll see you tomorrow and take care of you."

He said: "Look, they'll be down there about 11 P.M. and try to catch you coming out of Chiambi's joint."

"Okay," I said. "I won't forget this."

The call came about 6:30 P.M. I told Nicky and Chico about the warning. We were driving Patsy Fabiano's black convertible. Chico took the rifle and the shotgun out of the car and we stashed our handguns. The thought of the law coming out to get us when we were ready for them made us laugh, but we decided to cooperate. At exactly 11 P.M. we stepped out of Chiambi's place and got into the car. I spotted an unmarked cop car parked on Havre Street.

Still trying to cooperate, we drove down Bennington and headed for Day Square. All of a sudden we were in a lot of traffic and about to lose them, so we headed back to Chiambi's and parked out front. The law pulled up with tires screeching. They got out of their cars with guns drawn.

John Doyle, who worked with the district attorney's office, seemed to be in charge. He ordered: "Step out of the car."

I said: "What's this about?"

He said: "We want to shake you down."

I said: "With drawn guns? You motherfucker, I'm going to call my lawyer about this."

Billy McCarthy said: "All right, knock it off."

Detective Bobby Fawcett pushed Nicky up against the building. Fawcett was holding a pistol while he searched Nicky. He didn't find anything.

There were at least seven cops with guns in their hands. They searched us and the car and then they searched again, but in the end they left empty-handed. Thanks to the tip we were clean. I gave the tipster-cop $100.

Next to try were the state police.

I came out of Alphonso's with Nicky and Chico. A cop was standing there with a big, shiny chrome-plated gun in his hand. He said: "All right, Barboza, hold it right there."

I began shaking my knees and waving my hands up over my head. I said: "Oh please, Mista Police, sir, don't shoot poor little ole me with that great big ole gun."

The cop looked a little addled so I cut the comedy. "Put that thing away before it goes off, you mother-fucker," I said.

He didn't move and it was then I looked around and saw six state cops coming at me with drawn guns. What's more, there were ten others backing them up. One was crouched behind the hood of a car with a shotgun pointed at me. Another shotgunner was behind a telephone pole.

It was far out. I said: "What's this all about?"

One of the state cops said: "We have a warrant for your arrest on a charge of driving to endanger."

They put me in a police car and drove me to State Police Headquarters at 1010 Commonwealth Avenue. The TV cameras were all set up and waiting when we got there. A cop said:

"Put your coat over your head and we'll lead you."

"Yeah," I said. "Right into a telephone pole."

He said: "I promise you'll be all right."

"Okay," I said.

I went into headquarters with my black mohair coat over my head. Looking down, I could see the sidewalk. At 1 A.M. it looked like daylight because of all the flashbulbs.

They'd called in Detective John Hurley from Revere because they knew I trusted him. The place was loaded with cops from all over, all there to get a look at me. The state cop who had got the warrant for me was there. His name was Mario. I looked at him and realized what had happened.

"You punk," I said.

"That's enough, Joe," said Detective Hurley.

"Look, John," I said. "If that fat bastard didn't dress like a frustrated gangster with his black trench coat and black bomber, I wouldn't have thought it was somebody making a move on me when I saw him standing there in the dark beside his car. And I wouldn't have taken off the way I did. Hell, maybe I might have even stopped when the others chased me. Driving to endanger, my ass. He's just mad because they lost me."

Hurley didn't say anything so I kept talking. "Okay, I'll lose my driver's license over this, and that's cool. You guys could always see me coming before but I'll sell my James Bond car, as you call it, to John Fitzgerald—he wants it bad—

and from now on I'll use cabs and subways and other drivers. From now on you'll all work for your money."

Hurley just shook his head. I went to court and was put on $2,500 bond. Attorney Fitzgerald gave me $1,000 for my car.

No doubt about it, I was hot.

6

The Jackals Gather

Whether local police knew it or not—and the matter can be debated—their pressure on Joe Barboza worked to the advantage of the Mafia. Within a matter of a few days the world turned upside down for the stocky "Portugee." He was abruptly stripped of "strength" by men he had trusted in the past. To the shock of betrayal was added a heavy burden of grief. But even behind bars, Joe was not a man to push around and eventually he decided to push back.

1

I was sitting in the Intermission Lounge on Washington Street. It was November 5, 1966, and I wasn't carrying a gun. For the last two weeks I hadn't carried a gun. The gang war was over.

Detectives Knuckles Donovan and Horse Miller came in. I grabbed Knuckles and pretended to frisk him. He, in turn, frisked me. We got a big laugh out of it. I offered to buy them a drink but they refused because they were on duty.

I turned around and looked toward the door. A friend of mine was standing there and he was giving me the high sign. So I excused myself and went outside. The guy followed me and we went around the corner.

My friend told me that Romeo Gallo of the Gallo Mob in Brooklyn was in town with a contract to kill me. The Marfeo brothers had let the contract because they blamed me for Willie Marfeo's death recently in a phonebooth in Rhode Island.

It was a bum rap. More than a year ago Raymond had asked me to take care of Willie who was causing heat in Providence with his floating crap game. I was all ready to move on it when Raymond called it off. I hadn't heard any more about it until the other day when Raymond changed his mind again and brought in an out-of-towner to make the hit.

Now it occurred to me that maybe Raymond was up to something tricky. Maybe he was trying to get me killed for free by letting me be blamed for Willie's death. Well, fuck Romeo Gallo. He could die like anybody else. I went back inside the Intermission and stayed until closing time. I thought about borrowing a gun, just in case, but then I decided to hell with it.

Tashi, Nicky, Patsy and I came out together. We decided to go to Swartzie's in Revere for something to eat. We rode in Tashi's car, a gray Cadillac. As we headed down Washington Street we spotted a vice squad car following us. I told the boys to get rid of anything hot, and I personally threw out three joints of grass and two new addresses from Detroit and Florida. When we were stopped on Congress Street, we were clean.

Detective Linsky came up to the car and said: "All right, what's your name?"

"Go and fuck yourself," I said.

He said: "I'm only doing my job."

I said: "Go down to the South End and break those nigger junkies' balls."

He said: "Are you going to give me your name?"

I said: "Look, I was shook down by the state police at

two this afternoon in East Boston and at 12 midnight in the Intermission by Knuckles Donovan. If you want anything from me, take me to the station and I'll call my attorney."

He said: "I'm booking you all."

"For what?"

"Suspicion."

They put us in a paddy wagon, leaving the car parked against the curbstone. Tashi put some papers on the floor and burned them. Then he said: "I just remembered there's a .45 in the glove compartment."

I nearly leaped out of my seat. "What?"

He said: "I forgot that Tommy DiPrisco called this morning and asked me to bring the .45 along for him. He didn't ask for it and I forgot it was in there."

I said: "We had time to throw away a cannon, let alone a pistol. You realize the law will try to blame me?"

They brought us into headquarters and discovered I had $1,100 on me, but they were used to finding more. I refused to be fingerprinted.

"You've taken my fingerprints every week for the last two years," I said. "Go and fuck yourself tonight."

They didn't even try to make mug shots. Just kept stalling. Then a friend came over and told me they'd found the gun. I knew they had taken it without a search warrant, but all I could do was scream. They booked us for possession of a firearm. Later, in court, they claimed a "reliable informant" had tipped them I was on my way to make a hit, and that while following me they saw me pass a gun to Nicky to put away. The district attorney issued a statement and the newspapers had headlines two inches high: BARBOZA CALLED THE BIGGEST KILLER IN THE COMMONWEALTH.

This stirring statement made the chief justice put me on bail of $100,000 for possession of a gun.

Tashi and Fabiano got out but Nicky was held on $50,000 bail, and both of us ended up in the Charles Street Jail. Tashi,

Chico and DiPrisco went out collecting money. They even shook down people in their efforts to get me out. One night at the Coliseum, the after-hours joint run by Sammy Granito, DiPrisco had an argument and pushed Granito in the face. He got together with Larry Biaoni who had been responsible for Tashi Bratsos' brother's death twelve years before, and they went to Jerry Anguilo with some lies. Jerry went to Raymond and got an okay for a move on Tashi, DiPrisco and Chico.

Tashi came to me to report. He said they had all but $28,000 to get me and Nicky out, and the Office had promised to supply the difference. He predicted we'd be out in two days.

That night Tashi and DiPrisco walked into the Nite Lite Lounge which was operated by Ralphie Chong. Patsy Fabiano waited out in the car but nobody knew he was there. About 1:30 A.M. the last of the customers came out. But Tashi and DiPrisco didn't. And neither did twelve other men, all Office connected.

They shot Tashi and DiPrisco, and kicked DiPrisco in the head for pushing Granito. And they robbed them of all the money they had collected to get me out of jail.

Wimpy Bennett found out what had happened and he tipped the law. The law came in at 7 A.M. and found a bullet hole behind a new mirror. In the cellar they found bloody carpets. A new carpet had been laid in the lounge. On the sidewalk they found a man trying to wash away bloodstains. The blood had splattered when they put Tashi and DiPrisco in a car and dumped their bodies in South Boston.

The law couldn't prove who killed them, but they brought charges against Ralphie Chong for trying to cover up the crime. He pleaded guilty, expecting to get three to five years. Instead, after the FBI investigated a reported bribe, he got two sentences of from five to seven years, to run consecutively.

I couldn't get out on bail, and I was pretty sure I'd go back to Walpole. Well, anyway, I could wait for Ralphie there.

2

Following the murders of Tashi and DiPrisco, Chico called a meeting of our friends. The meeting was held in a South Boston poolroom. Wimpy Bennett was there and so was Steve Flemmi, Frank Salanni, John and Jimmy Marteranno and Jimmy Kearns.

There was a lot of talk, from what Chico told me later, and everybody was making threats and feeling everybody else out. Finally, Chico got fed up with all the crap and he came right out and asked: "What are we going to do about it?"

There was more talk before Wimpy took it on himself to answer Chico. Wimpy said: "Nobody wants to take on the Office. Not right now, anyway. They want to sit back and see what happens."

Chico just looked at him in disgust. Wimpy took him to one side and said: "I know how you can win them over. The Office only has two killers—Larry Biaoni and Phil Wagonheimer. If you'll kill Larry, I'll arrange to take care of Phil. He'll run to Florida when Larry's hit and I can have him taken care of down there."

"Will the others go along then?" Chico asked.

"They'll be with you after you make the move on Biaoni," Wimpy said. "I guarantee it."

It made some sense, but Chico didn't trust Wimpy. Biaoni was about the best killer the Office had, and Wimpy hated his guts. Chico suspected some double-dealing. He turned to the others and asked: "Is that the way you feel?"

Nobody said anything, willing to let Wimpy do their talking. Wimpy said: "They'll be with you after you make a move on Biaoni."

Chico didn't know what else to do so he and Kearns left and began casing Biaoni. They sat outside the Bat Cave on Friend Street; they checked his club in Chinatown; they watched the bar he worked out of in the South End; they went to his home in Franklin and peeped through the windows.

In the Charles Street Jail, I was boiling mad at Wimpy. Like the sneaky weasel he was, he was trying to use Chico to kill Biaoni. Chico promised in one letter he smuggled into me: "I'm going to do my best, Joe, but if I die I want you to cut that motherfucker's head off and put it on my grave."

And then Louis Grieco, who had helped me in the Deegan hit, and my old partner Guy Frizzi joined against me. Guy sent Patsy Fabiano into a trap in Chelsea where Grieco was waiting, but Patsy did some fast driving and got away.

On Pearl Harbor Day, 1966, Chico and Kearns went into a belly-dancing lounge owned by Biaoni. Larry wasn't there but one of his relatives was. Chico slapped him hard and said: "That's for Larry."

On the way out, Chico mentioned they were going to Alphonso's Lounge in Revere. Somebody got on a phone. When Chico and Kearns got there they found Guy and Benny. They sat together for fifteen minutes and then Chico and Kearns left. As they were leaving, Benny—who with Mario and the Pig had killed their partner, Rocco DeSeglio, on Jerry Anguilo's orders—went to one of the windows. He pushed aside the curtains and rapped hard on the window. Down on the street, men were sitting in a car. They got the message. Benny then came back to Guy and lifted his glass in a toast: "Well," he said, "that's the last you'll see of Chico."

Guy, who had introduced Chico to me in 1962 as a "good kid," sat there and didn't do anything.

Down below, Chico and Kearns got into their car. Kearns was driving. They headed out of the parking lot to the artery circle to take a ramp to the highway. Following behind was a car with Wisconsin plates. Holding the rifle was the Pig. Mario was driving.

The first shot went through the window in the rear and

through the back of Chico's head. He slumped over dead. The bullet didn't pass through his head but pushed his eyes forward. There was a lump on his lower front forehead where everything was pushed forward. More bullets plowed through the car, splintering into fine bits of shrapnel. Kearns was hit in the back. He continued to drive, zigzagging all over the road until he finally went over the embankment and into a field.

About 3 A.M. I was awakened in my cell in the Charles Street Jail and taken downstairs to the lawyer's conference room. Detectives George Hurley and Mickey Consolla were waiting for me. Hurley said: "We've got some bad news for you, Joe."

I looked at him. I was used to friends dying and I knew he was going to tell me somebody was dead.

He told me what happened to Chico. I just sat stunned. No matter who died it affected me, but Chico's death affected me the worse. He was like my son, my brother, my partner. Finally I said: "Get Patsy Fabiano off the street. He don't know how to handle himself against these type of people and they'll kill him." "

Okay," said Detective Hurley.

I went back to my cell and told Nicky. Fabiano was put in Dedham Jail. In time he was brought to the Charles Street Jail.

Kearns was brought in, all bandaged up. We talked.

From my cell I could see the whole guardroom and see who entered and left. But, of course, it worked both ways. Nicky and I were in that cell so they could always watch us. Within a few days I spotted Attorney Joe Balliro. I sent down word I'd like to speak to him. He called me down and was very remorseful over Tashi Bratsos' death because, he said, he liked Tashi.

I said: "You tell Jerry he's not getting away with this. Anything goes."

Balliro said: "I'll tell him, but are you sure you want me to?"

I said: "You're motherfucking right I want you to tell him."

He came back a couple of days later and said: "Jerry swears he had nothing to do with what happened to Tashi, DiPrisco and Chico. Jerry said it is a terrible mess and he has a problem getting the twenty-six thousand Tashi owed him. That's the only thing he's concerned about—his money."

I didn't say anything more. It was useless to talk to Balliro. He hero-worshipped Anguilo. What's more, his, own cousin, Frankie Balliro, was in the Nite Lite when Tashi and Tommy got it. He also didn't know that Jerry had gone to Rhode Island and spent a day getting an okay to move against me in the jail. Raymond refused until Jerry said: "Why am I giving you money if I can't get protection?" When he saw he was about to lose his biggest trick, Raymond finally said it was okay to hit me.

No, there was no use to talk to Balliro, but there were others I might talk to later.

3

In January, 1967, I went to Walpole to join the Bear. Nicky came with me. We got four to five years. Fabiano went to Deer Island.

I said to the Bear: "Wimpy is a treacherous sick buzzard."

The Bear said: "Don't worry about it. You'll be happy soon. Just watch."

A week later I was in Block One of the maximum section watching TV with Nicky and Jimmy Marteranno. The Bear came in and said: "Joe, I want to speak to you. Alone."

We went down to the end of the block and the Bear said: "Wimpy is dead."

I said: "How, when, who did it?"

The Bear said: "It happened this way. Wimpy told Frank Salanni that when I got out they'd better kill me because I'd cause too much trouble. He told Frank not to tell my brother, Stevie, but Frank did tell Stevie and Stevie went insane."

I waited. The Bear continued: "Wimpy was in a garage with two men. One of them told Wimpy: 'You rat,' and shot him under the right eye. Then they buried Wimpy."

"So Wimpy the Fox is dead?" I said.

The Bear said: "The fox that bit us is dead."

Within a week the press began to run stories about how Wimpy was missing, believed dead, and then more stories about how he was involved in the Brink's robbery and how he had visited Specs O'Keefe and tried to bribe him not to testify against the Brink's bandits.

To this day Wimpy's body hasn't been found.

Walter Bennett went searching for his brother. He got too close to the truth. They strangled him in a house in Dorchester and buried him right near Wimpy. As they had done with Wimpy, they covered the body with lime. The Bear used to laugh and say: "Wimpy and Walter are together playing whist."

Billy Bennett, the third brother, went looking. He got too close and was killed too, but he was left where he could be found. It annoyed the Bear. He said: "Dammit. I wish they'd buried him with the other two so Wimpy and Walter could have had a referee when they play whist. Nothing like keeping it in the family."

4

When I went back to Walpole I went back as kitchen manager and runner, a job that let me travel all over the prison at my leisure. Ralphie Chong was still out on bail on account of the Nite Lite incident, but I knew it was just a matter of time.

One day I heard that Ralphie had been brought in. I went

down to see him. He was standing there in a t-shirt, shorts and socks looking gnome-like as ever. When he saw me he said: "Joe, you know I always liked you and did everything I could for you. What happened wasn't my fault. I had no say in the matter. Why, they even used me to take the beef."

I said: "Ralphie, I know you're my friend. I don't hold no grudge. Tommy asked for what he got. I just want the beef straightened out so I won't have no worry later."

Officer Joe Bobbin came up and told me I'd have to leave but I could see Ralphie upstairs. I smiled and said okay. Then I went out the door and leaned against the wall while my body trembled with rage. I told myself I'd make that little gnome tell me everything.

That evening I walked into Block #8, the new men's block which was also one of the TV sections. Ralphie was standing against the wall with ass-kissers all around him.

"I want to talk to you, Ralphie," I said.

The ass-kissers left without being told. I continued: "Look, to show you I'm your friend I'll tell you a secret. I've got some powerful tasteless poison. I've also got a zip gun. You let me know who is bothering you or who you want killed and I'll take care of them."

Ralphie looked scared, but he said: "Okay, Joe. Thanks."

He kept looking at me hard and thinking a mile a minute. I walked away laughing hard on the inside. I didn't have no poison, but I did have a plan. I'd have this little bastard brought down to his real level by the time I was ready to pounce on him.

Next day we had stuffed pork chops. I was passing them out on the side Ralphie came in on. When he came by, I said: "Look, Ralphie, I saved you two nice big ones."

Ralphie said: "No, thanks, Joe, I'm not hungry."

It went on like that for the next few days. Ralphie wouldn't accept any food from me. He kept saying: "I'm not hungry." Then finally, after starving, he'd say: "No, not that big piece. Give me this little one in the corner." And I'd look sad as if he'd loused up my chance to poison him and say: "Okay, Ralphie."

Then he stopped eating entirely. I found out that Tony Pino, one of the Brink's bandits, was feeding him from the warehouse. I went to Pino and warned him to stop. For good measure I added: "You're always talking about Raymond. Well, your name happened to come up in conversation one day in Raymond's office, and he said he'd never met you."

I had guys checking Ralphie's cell and I found out he took regular naps in the afternoon and was locked in. During the 3 P.M. unlock, which was also the time to change the guards, there was a lot of confused hustling and running around by guards. The next Tuesday I waited until 3 o'clock for all the confusion to begin. I heard the cell doors open. I got into Ralphie's cell while he was still on his bunk and moved in between the sink and the head of the bed. Ralphie opened his eyes and saw me. His eyes got wider when he saw the meat cleaver in my belt. I said: "Don't flinch or move your hands. I know you got a knife under your pillow but before you can reach it I'll sink this cleaver into your greasy head."

Ralphie said: "What's the matter?"

I said: "Tell me what happened at the Nite Lite." Ralphie Chong, who had refused to answer to the law, told me who was there that night, who fired the shots, who did the kicking.

A couple of convicts came to the cell as he was talking. They left when I said: "Get out of here."

When he was through telling me, I said: "I'm going to kill you, but not now. I want you to worry, but I swear I'll kill you."

I spat on him and left.

Ralphie had visitors the next day. He told his visitors. They went to the politicians and he was transferred the following day. I watched him as he walked down the corridor with his laundry basket full of his belongings. As he passed me, he put down his head and walked faster. Going to Norfolk Prison two miles down the hill.

Scared shitless.

5

Not long after Chong left for Norfolk, I was talking to Joe Devlin, an ex-fighter. Officer James Tanish paged me on the speaker. I went to the control room and Tanish said: "Two FBI agents want to talk to you."

I said: "Tell them to go fuck themselves."

I walked away about fifty feet, then turned around and said: "I'll see them."

Hell, I thought, maybe I'll find out something.

When I got out in the visiting room, one agent said: "I'm Paul Rico and this is Denny Condon."

I said: "I've met you before, Rico. At the track. Do you go there often?"

He said: "No, I don't gamble."

Then I sat back and listened to what they had to say. I sat there listening and the thought I'd been playing with in my subconscious mind came back. What do I owe those people at the Office? They killed Chico, Tashi, DiPrisco, took $82,000 of money meant to bail me out, tried to kill Patsy Fabiano three times, helped frame me into the can on this four to five I'm doing, talked Pearson into testifying against me so I face twenty years on that charge, muscled into my shylock business, intimidated witnesses favoring me and so forth. The Living Room that I had hustled was now paying the Office weekly to support Ralphie Chong's family. They were doing everything in their power to keep me in prison.

Yes, they would never let me out if they could stop it. They know they'd have to kill me if I got out and they know I'd take plenty of them with me. That old fool in Rhode Island misinterpreted my respect for fear. Fear him? I didn't fear tougher guys than Raymond Patriarca. Besides, I'd learned to accept dying a long time ago as my friends all around me died in the gang war.

I've got nothing left but my mouth with which to fight now. I'd be a fool to keep quiet on the theory that twenty years from now, when I'm 55, I could get out and get even. No, now while I'm young is the time to get even. I'll bring them in the can with me since I can't get out to them, and when I get them here we'll get on with it.

Rico and Condon were silent now, looking at me. I said: "All right, I'll give you some information."

They just looked at me. They didn't believe me, but they had to go along with the game until their cynicism was confirmed. Rico told me later: "You had a deadpan expression on your face all the while I talked to you. I couldn't read any sign that I was reaching you."

At the time I just said: "I want protection for my wife and children."

They both said: "Your wife and children will have it."

7

At Bay

Newspaper writers were quick to compare Joe Barboza to Joe Valachi when news of his counterattack was leaked to them. Instantly there was a press buildup patterned after the one given to Valachi in 1963. There were the usual stories of a price on the informer's head and much semi-official speculation about the regional and national impact of his tales on "La Cosa Nostra." But all the sensationalism couldn't obscure the fact that Barboza was talking of current events, not of ancient history, and his testimony, unlike Valachi's fairy tales, could send men to prison. Perhaps it was because Barboza needed no press agent that he soon became disgusted with the games press and politicians played.

Special Agents Rico and Condon wanted to know what I had on Raymond. He was their number one target. Among other things I told them about the Marfeo business.

Willie Marfeo had been running this crap game over a package store in the Federal Hill section of Providence. He was told by Raymond and Henry to close it down. The last time Henry told him to close, Willie pushed Henry in the face and called him an "asshole." Willie added: "You people want a loaf of bread and then you throw the crumbs back. Well, fuck you; I ain't closing down."

The police went to Raymond and told him the game was causing too much interest and to get it closed or they'd start raiding all the points on the Hill. Raymond knew he couldn't afford to let this happen, so he sent for me and Ronnie. Henry was there too. Raymond ran down the whole history of the situation. When he implied he'd pay us well to take care of Willie, I told him I'd do it for nothing.

Henry said: "I told you he was a good kid."

Raymond said: "I won't forget this, Joe."

Then we talked about what we'd use to make the move. Raymond said he'd supply everything, even a meat truck. His idea was for us to use a meat truck with us dressed in white smocks with hats and pushing a dolly loaded with meat into a store. When we got to the sidewalk we'd whack out Willie.

After we left Raymond, Henry showed us a couple of places Marfeo frequented. On the way back to Boston Ronnie and I talked. He remembered a time when Henry double-crossed a couple of guys who were pulling a stickup job. The men were killed by the law. I figured maybe we'd better stall a little so I went back to Rhode Island alone and told Henry I wanted some pictures of Marfeo. He told me Raymond wanted to see me. Raymond said the hit was off for awhile. The law had heard about the beef Willie had with Henry.

A year went by and I didn't hear nothing more about Marfeo. It was just after I got out of Deer Island on that disturbing the peace rap that Connie Frizzi ran up and said: "You hear about Willie Marfeo getting killed in a telephone booth over in Rhode Island?"

I drove out to Arthur's Farm to see Henry and find out what happened. We went into the back of the store and Henry said: "We reached out for a good man. He found Willie in this restaurant. All the customers in it were our people. The hit man took Willie over to a phonebooth and filled him full of lead."

Later on, as I've already described, Raymond told Willie's

brothers that I was the hit man and they sent Romeo Gallo after me but the law got me first.

That was the story. Rico and Condon liked it and so did Paul Markham and Ted Harrington. Markham was a close friend of Senator Edward Kennedy and he was United States attorney in Boston. Ted was younger, a lanky Irishman out of Fall River. He had worked with the organized crime section of Justice back in the old days of Bobby Kennedy. Now he was an assistant United States attorney under Markham. Ted was straight as they come and he had a sense of humor and did he like to eat! Later on I cooked a lot of spaghetti for him and he couldn't ever get enough. Markham was all right, but basically he was a politician. I liked Harrington and it was good I did because he did most of the work with me.

Right off they grabbed on the Marfeo angle because it gave them a federal handle. The fact that Raymond had called interstate, and I had traveled from Boston to Providence gave them jurisdiction under a new law that Bobby Kennedy had sponsored. The law made it a federal crime to cross a state line in aid of racketeering—and murder was racketeering, the way they saw it. The fact that I didn't kill Marfeo wasn't important. I was part of a conspiracy to kill him.

The Deegan and DeSeglio hits, for example, didn't have any federal angle. They told me they would arrange for me to testify later to the state grand jury on those cases.

After I testified in secret before the federal grand jury, I was transferred to the Barnstable County Jail on Cape Cod and held in protective custody. I was upstairs, all alone in the women's section. Rico and Condon were there every day to ask more questions. One thing they asked me about was the murder of Jackie Francioni. They let me see a transcript of a tape recording of a conversation on Raymond's telephone in Providence. Raymond was talking to Henry and he asked him who killed Francioni. Henry blamed me.

I laughed and told them the story as it had been told to me. A guy named Frank was mad at Francioni over some cheating with a numbers ticket. One day Francioni was shoveling snow from around his car when Frank walked down the hill to him. They went into Francioni's basement apartment. Francioni was in front. When Francioni got into the middle of the room, Frank pulled a gun and shot him in the back of the head. The impact threw Francioni across the room to the corner. Frank leaned over him and fired two more times in his head and left.

The landlord was upstairs with a bad cold. He said he heard the three shots and then a voice say: "Stop playing with those firecrackers, Jackie."

After awhile the landlord went downstairs and found Jackie dead.

That was the story and, like the truth about a lot of killings, it was one thing to know what happened and something else to have first-hand knowledge a court would accept.

It was funny about those tapes the FBI had, though. Shortly after I saw that transcript, the whole damned thing was made public. It happened over in Rhode Island. Louis "the Fox" Taglianetti was fighting a tax case and his lawyers moved that the FBI turn over all records of their investigation. Much to everyone's surprise, this thick file of wiretaps on Raymond's phone was produced and put into the public record. The defense claimed the taps "tainted" the evidence against Louis, and maybe they did because the taps were illegal. Yet everybody forgot all about Taglianetti in the uproar over the secret tapes and the newspapers had a field day. Some of them censored out a few names like Joe Linsey, of course, and nobody said a word about the FBI breaking the law. Naturally.

Three years after the tapes were brought out, in 1970, Taglianetti took this girl home. He left her at the door. She went inside. Somebody gunned the Fox to death. The girl came back outside to look and she was gunned down too. But nobody could blame the gang war. It had been over for years.

To get back to May, 1967, when the tapes were published. It created a sensation, like I said. The Boston *Sunday Advertiser* came out with a story saying: "Raymond Patriarca's long reign as boss of the Cosa Nostra family in New England may have been ended by the disclosure of how deeply the FBI was able to penetrate his organization, the *Sunday Advertiser* learned Saturday. . . ."

It was a good buildup, I guess, for what came a few days later. Because of my testimony a federal grand jury indicted Raymond Patriarca, Henry Tameleo and Ronnie Casesso for interstate transportation of hoodlums to conspire to murder Willie Marfeo. Not the murder of Willie, you understand, but an attempt in which a conspiracy to murder was alleged. It was the biggest breakthrough into organized crime in New England history. The federal government had found somebody who wasn't afraid to testify against the Mafia boss of New England. Headlines screamed about the sensational charges brought by the "Songbird," the "Canary," the "Turncoat." That's what they called me.

I used to cry when I read what they were calling me. Why?—I would ask with blurry eyes. Why? They shout for law and order, they pressure the police for action, but when they're handed on a silver platter somebody willing to stand up and do what most Americans are afraid to do, they call him names. Don't they realize that these names of "Songbird" and "Canary" only help organized crime by discouraging other potential witnesses from coming forward? What is it they really want?

Slowly I realized that the entire news network is only interested in money. They thrive like leeches off the misery and suffering of others. I dare anybody to answer differently. Freedom of the press is abused daily by the money-hungry news media.

John Fitzgerald became my sole lawyer after I refused to have anything to do with other lawyers the Mafia could pressure. After the Patriarca indictment came through, John came down to the Barnstable Jail to see me. I gave him a list of names and said: "You tell these people and the Office that if they don't undo the wrongs they've done me, I'll testify against them. Tell them they'd better let me out so they can kill me because if they don't I'm going to testify against them. Tell them I also want fifty thousand dollars."

Fitzgerald said: "I'll deliver the message, Joe."

Raymond sent back word he'd put the money in escrow. I said: "Tell him to go and fuck his mother. I want it now or no deal."

It was no deal. Raymond's lawyers had meetings and advised Raymond I couldn't hurt him or anybody else. I appeared before the Suffolk county grand jury on two occasions. The first time they indicted Jerry Anguilo, the Pig, Benny and Mario for the DeSeglio murder. The second time they indicted Tameleo, Peter Limone, Ronnie Casesso, Louis Grieco, Joe Salvati, Roy French and Joe Barboza. That was the Deegan case, of course, and it was understood I'd plead guilty and testify for the state and get a suspended sentence.

All this sold a lot of newspapers and gave them new chances to talk about "Barboza the Songbird." Word came back to me that the Office was screaming for my life and offering $300,000 to the man who killed me. It didn't bother me much. I had accepted dying too long to worry about it now.

A reporter wanted to write a book about me, and we talked it over. He had shown a lot of courage in his column, but suddenly he backed off the book and asked for police protection. The Office had threatened his life, he said.

All this time the pressure grew on the sheriff and my guards at Barnstable. It was decided to move me after I had finished testifying to the grand juries. Late one night I was taken to a little airport and turned over to federal marshals. They put me on a Coast Guard seaplane and flew me to Logan Airport in East Boston. The marshals put me in a car and started to the Federal Building on Congress Street. As we entered the tunnel I noticed a car following us. I told the marshals and they put out an alert. The car followed us to the Federal Building where it was stopped and was found to contain reporters who had been tipped off by somebody at the airport. The marshals asked how I knew we were being followed and I told them: "It's my business to notice such things."

I spent the night at the marshals' office and got acquainted with Robert Morey. He turned out to be one of the classiest men I ever met in the entire political structure. Next day I was flown to Thatcher's Island off the coast from Gloucester. It was isolated, lonely and had only two houses on it, both of which were used by the Coast Guard.

It didn't take me long to learn to hate the place. There was a foghorn that blew every thirty seconds in foggy weather, which was quite frequent. There was poison ivy all over the island and deep holes that if you fell into you would break your neck. There were rats and snakes. It was a real hellhole.

Every two weeks a new detail of marshals would be brought out to relieve the twelve men on duty. The boat went to and from the island regularly with men and supplies. My wife and child went on some of the trips to shop and visit since the island was too lonely for them. Lights could be seen on the island from shore and people in Gloucester were wondering what was happening out there.

At first I avoided the marshals and didn't realize a power struggle was building but then I started playing cards with them and got to know what was going on. I liked John Partington who set me up a sandbag and a speedbag so I could work out. There were some fine marshals on the detail but there were the drunks, the shirkers and the troublemakers too. These last were politically hungry and hoped to use me to help their careers.

All this time the press was looking for me and eventually they found me. There were pictures on TV and in the papers of "Baron's Island," and stories about the marshals guarding me and details that could only help the Office. Then the feds got word that the Mafia had bought sixteen hundred pounds of dynamite and was going to blow up the island and everybody on it. That story got into the papers too.

The news media which demanded law and order had revealed my hiding place with the excuse of keeping the public informed. What did the public care? In doing so they threatened the lives of a woman, her little baby, and twelve U.S. marshals. How sick can you get?

I was moved to an estate on the shore line on the other side of Gloucester. The estate was valued at $480,000, but it was furnished like houses I've seen in slum areas. There were four big houses on the estate with fences making a closed compound, and it was right next to a Coast Guard station which made it an ideal security post. There was just one problem— a newspaperman lived in a house next to the estate. The marshals made a deal with him—if he kept quiet they'd let him print the story first when the time came. The marshal detail was increased to twenty men.

The estate was turned into a fortress. Barbed wire was strung along the sea side and flare bombs were attached to trip wires out in the woods. I had three shepherd dogs I trained to circle the whole estate every hour and to run inside the fence by the road when cars came by. I set up a lighting system with spotlights that made it impossible to get near the houses without being seen.

But there was still a problem with some of the men. Once I found the corner of my house unattended and I stood under the window of my bedroom for forty minutes with a revolver in my pocket and a flashlight in my hand. I did this to prove that the marshal detail sometimes let my family down.

During the time I stayed at the estate I amused my self by training my dog Zero. He became like a dog you see in the movies. He could heel, sit, lay down, crawl, roll over, jump over my back, catch balls and sticks, fetch, speak and a lot of other things. When I said "check" he would check the perimeter of the estate. If I touched the back of his ear he would charge at any person near me, but he wouldn't bite anybody unless I told him to. Minus, my other dog, was cuckoo like all females and if you even hollered at me or the baby she'd rip your pants off—as two of the marshals found out.

I played cards with the marshals and ping-pong. We fished a lot. I cooked many big meals for the marshals who were liable to go hungry at times if I didn't. Over three hundred marshals from the four corners of the United States served on the detail and I made friends with many of them. No two were closer than John Partington and Bud Warren. Bud was from North Dakota and won a Grand National pistol and rifle shooting contest. Concerned citizens should be proud of the marshals. They are thoroughly abused and underpaid. But isn't that the way of America—kick the good and let the bad get away with their evil?

Once Partington and I came back from checking the woods on the estate and we saw about eight marshals hiding behind trees and looking toward this swimming pool on the adjacent property. I looked through the binoculars and saw a photographer taking posed pictures of this broad in the nude. I also saw a lot of Coast Guard men watching with binoculars from trees and bushes. She had an unseen audience of about twenty-five men as the photographer took bust shots, beaver shots and shots with her behind sticking up toward the moon. She was a pretty girl and the photographer was sweating. It was quite a show while it lasted.

All this time I was conferring with Harrington and with the district attorney's people, and later I was testifying at the trials. They had to sneak me in by a different route each time. Once I was taken in a Coast Guard cutter to the foot of Hanover Street in the middle of the night. Another time I was brought in on a fishing boat and picked up at the South Boston pier. Once they took me in by mail truck and delivered me to the post office in the Federal Building. On another occasion I was brought in by helicopter. We landed near the Charles River and I ran across a field to a car with a small army of machine gun-toting federal marshals guarding me.

Every time I testified, I was kept in the courthouse until I was finished. I was on the stand in the Patriarca case three days, five days on the DeSeglio case and nine days on the Deegan case. While I was in the courthouse, guards patrolled the corridors at night with police dogs. There were patrols outside the building too. Marshals slept in the courthouse with me. I even had an official food taster by the name of Deputy Marshal George Hayes. A man let himself be arrested in an effort to figure out how he could hit me in the courthouse. A police officer's uniform was stolen. The room I stayed in at the Suffolk Courthouse was secured with sheets of steel over the windows to stop snipers or bombtossers. The Office finally decided that it was impossible to hit me and the newspaper made a story out of what they called "Mission Impossible."

When I left the courthouse, decoy cars went first. Once I was dressed like a marshal and carrying a M-1 rifle while I pretended to guard Jesse Gerder who was pretending to be me. We sneaked out a side entrance. I blew it though. I couldn't resist saying to Gerder: "All right, Barboza, you asshole, keep moving." That brought a roar from everybody and some cop saw my face under the hood and talked. Of course the newspapers got hold of it.

Shortly after I came to the estate another writer agreed to write the book. He was soon under pressure from the Office. John Fitzgerald, my lawyer, was catching hell too. I warned him the Office would kill him, but John had too much guts to quit. He was asked to meet with Larry Biaoni at a Howard Johnson restaurant just outside Boston. He was smart enough to tip off Attorney General Elliott Richardson who had the meeting staked out. They saw Phil Wagonheimer in the middle of the parking lot where Fitzgerald met with Biaoni. Larry offered to help John. This was typical of the Mafia. Anytime they wanted something they would pressure the person and cause him trouble. Then a Mafia figure would step in and offer to help. The pressure would stop and the victim would be indebted to the Mafia. I had helped Henry Tameleo pull the same stunt when he was trying to get control of the License Board in Revere. Fitzgerald was aware of this technique and he told Biaoni: "You tell that diabetic asshole in Rhode Island that if he don't lay off me, I'll testify myself."

Fitzgerald refused to be taken into protective custody but sometimes he'd let a couple of detectives see him home from court. One day while he was crossing the street a speeding car tried to run him down. Fitz scrambled aside, but I could see the handwriting on the wall. I figured maybe the Office should see it too.

Jerry Anguilo got a telegram which said: "Mene, mene, tekel upharsin."

It was signed: "The Animal."

The message was from the Bible and it meant: "You have been judged and found wanting. Your empire shall be handed to the Philistine."

Right after that the trial of Jerry and the others began. Toward the end of the trial the subject of my book came up. Here's how one newspaper told it: "At the trial, a defense counsel, Joseph Balliro, asked Barboza if he had been negotiating to sell his life story. Barboza said he was. The name of author Truman Capote, who wrote the best seller *In Cold Blood*, was mentioned. So was the name of *Boston Record American* columnist Harold Banks. Then Balliro asked Barboza if he had talked about the life story with his attorney. He said he had. Balliro asked Fitzgerald to stand up and asked Barboza if he were the man. Barboza said Fitzgerald was."

Now the heat was really on Fitzgerald. The Office had confirmed I was going to write a book. It figured the way to stop it was to get my lawyer who was arranging things.

The fact that the district attorney's office fouled up the case and Jerry got acquitted didn't help none. Jerry walked out on January 18, 1968, a free man. He told reporters: "I was in the Navy during the Second World War. Now I know what I was fighting for. I want to go home to my poor old mother."

Twelve days later Fitzgerald turned on his ignition and a bomb went off in his car.

It was my old James Bond car which I had sold to Fitzgerald. He was carrying two guns that day, yet for some reason he forgot to set the alarm when he parked the car. It was raining that day and the alarm was set with a key outside the car. Maybe John just didn't want to stop in the rain long enough to fumble with a key. He had always figured they'd come after him with guns anyway.

A little after 5 P.M. he left his office and went back to the car. Luckily, he followed his usual method of leaving the door open and his left foot out while he touched the accelerator with his right foot and, turned on the ignition. Having the door partly open saved his life.

Two sticks of dynamite weighing eight pounds exploded. Fitzgerald's legs were mangled. Windows were blown out in the house across the street. A cop who had been directing traffic close by was the first man on the scene. Fitzgerald was still in the driver's seat. He was bleeding from his face and his legs were mashed. But he was conscious. He told the cop:

"Call Rico of the FBI."

Fitzgerald was rushed to Whidden Memorial Hospital. A team of surgeons worked for five hours. They amputated John's right leg just below the knee, and they patched up the other leg which had been partly out of the car. All the hospital's supply of blood was used up during the operation and fresh blood had to be brought in from the Red Cross.

When I heard about it I went insane with fury. Deputy Marshal John Partington warned his men to be less concerned about people getting in and more concerned about me getting out. That's exactly what I was thinking about—getting out and going to a house in Everett and killing the man responsible. I was pretty sure who it was.

The TV and newspapers loved it. They screamed about law and order and how a lawyer, the father of five and the son of a minister, wasn't safe. The politicians all got into the act. They had pretty much ignored the gang war all those years with the excuse it was just punks, killing off punks and good riddance, but now that a lawyer had been maimed and crippled they rose up in wrath and tried to outdo each other in pious indignation.

I had to go into federal court for a pretrial hearing. Raymond sat in the back of the courtroom and looked at me. It was supposed to upset me. When I left the courtroom Raymond whispered to me: "You rat."

I said: "You fuck your dead mother in the mouth," and lunged at him. With a little luck I'd saved the government the cost of a trial, but the marshals grabbed me off my feet and carried me away.

The day of the trial came. A wheelchair sat outside the courtroom. The Office thought it was for Fitzgerald and its people were sweating. Two could play at psychological warfare. John never testified but I did. A Rhode Island official got on the stand as a character witness and said he had always found Mr. Patriarca to be a gentleman. The jury believed me. Patriarca, Tameleo and Casesso were found guilty and sentenced to five years and a $10,000 fine each.

The Deegan case finally came up. Statopoulos the Greek followed me on the stand and was solid as a rock. They couldn't shake him. Then came a surprise witness, a convict named Robert Glavin. He told how the Office offered him $50,000 to confess to the Deegan murder. The money was to be put in "escrow" and he was promised help in making parole when the new administration came in. Glavin had reported this at the time to the FBI and was told to play along and get all the information he could.

That was sensational enough but it was nothing compared to the day when Fitzgerald appeared in that wheelchair and testified about a $25,000 bribe offer to me. The offer was raised to $50,000 and the promise to "whack out Arthur Pearson" if necessary.

Fitzgerald told the court that he relayed the offer to me and then reported back: "Barboza said: 'Go to hell.'"

It took the jury seven hours and five minutes to find all six of the defendants guilty. Tameleo, Grieco, Limone and Casesso were sentenced to death. French and Salvati were given life imprisonment. The *Boston Globe's* story concluded: "Testimony in the case has probably been some of the most sensational ever heard."

It was just the beginning. People who had observed me testify and live another day began swamping the FBI with information. Other informers came forward to tell about Raymond and the Office. One of them was Red Kelly who told the world that if there had never been a Barboza there wouldn't have been a Kelly. Patriarca got ten more years.

Newsweek magazine printed a story and so did *Reader's Digest.* I was all over the national magazines. Walter Barnes, head of the Special Strike Force in Boston, who had worked closely with Markham and Harrington, told me: "Joe, you started all this."

The Gloucester newspaperman who lived near the estate was screaming to break the story. I was flown to Fort Knox, Kentucky, and hidden there with all the gold. It was something to think about.

It was at Fort Knox that the guard detail began falling apart. Security was at a minimum. Some of the marshals weren't exactly high caliber. I chased one from South Dakota up the stairs when I found him drunk on duty. I cut all the tires on one marshal's car when he turned out to be the most no-class creep of them all. I came just short of a deep breath of stabbing one marshal who went into my bedroom and took a book out of it. I got caught up in Rhode Island politics when Attorney General Herbert DeSimone wanted to try Patriarca on state charges growing out of the Marfeo case. The feds didn't want him to get any credit and they knocked DeSimone to me. One marshal said I should wait until after the election so it wouldn't help DeSimone.

Things got worse in 1969 when the Republicans took over the government. Markham and Harrington being Democrats were out of a job. I screamed so loud that Walter Barnes, head of the Strike Force in Boston, called me up and said he had been able to get Ted Harrington a job as his assistant and for me to shut up. Ted later became head of the Strike Force. His being there helped a little but not much because the Republicans hated me because I had helped the Democrats get Patriarca. Without having anything to do with it, I became a political football and got shafted. The Republicans didn't feel responsible for things the Democrats had promised to do for me. It was a nightmare.

Finally the Republicans decided that anything after Patriarca would be an anticlimax and they didn't need to keep me on ice any more. I was flown back from Fort Knox to Boston. Attorney Fitzgerald, with one leg and a cane, represented me. All court charges against me were filed away. That included the year and a day I'd been given for my part in the Deegan murder. Judge Felix Forte suspended the sentence. Then I appeared before the state parole board which okayed my release on all charges for which I'd been convicted. I was told to leave Massachusetts and never come back. It was March 28, 1969.

There was one final bit of misdirection. The reporter who had agreed to write my life story when the first one backed out cooperated. Later on he got scared off too, but at the time he came out with a long feature which reviewed my career in detail—sort of a preview of the book he hoped to write. His article ended like this: "And then Joe Barboza left Boston on an airplane headed for Europe, courtesy of the U.S. Government."

Actually, I flew to California with my wife and two children. I was given a new name and a new Social Security card, and I was enrolled in a cooking school where I learned French-style cooking. Mostly how to cook with wines. I graduated as a sauce, vegetable and roast cook, and I shipped out on the *S.S. President Wilson* bound for the Orient. So the reporter had been right about me leaving the country, even if I went in the other direction. It seemed hard to believe but I was about as far from Boston as I could get.

Part III

Trapped

Joe Barboza doesn't exaggerate when he describes the impact his testimony had on Boston-area crime. It can only be compared to what happened in New York in the late 1930's when Abe Reles "sang" about the inner workings of Murder, Inc. Eventually Reles died violently—"the canary who could sing but couldn't fly"—but not before scores of punks, big and little, decided to drop by the District Attorney's office "and cut myself a piece of cake."

It was under Attorney General Robert F. Kennedy that the value of encouraging informers was recognized and legal machinery was set up to provide means of protecting them. But with the death of President Kennedy, the war on organized crime lagged and the machinery was given little use. Assistant United States Attorney Edward F. Harrington had served under Bob Kennedy and was familiar with the legislation. When, thanks to Special Agents Rico and Condon, Barboza decided to make a deal, Harrington handled the arrangements.

Men who followed subsequent developments closely say that the importance of Barboza cannot be overestimated. Barboza was widely known to the underworld of Boston as an enemy of law enforcement. That federal and state officials could turn such an enemy into an ally impressed a lot of people. Moreover, the fact that he was protected while testifying against the most powerful gangster in New England was dramatic evidence of the government's power. In an area where corruption had become a way of life, the inability of the underworld to "reach" Barboza's protectors caused a lot of cynical people to revise their prejudices. Finally, the fact that the government kept its word to Barboza and did relocate him as promised was conclusive.

The "lesson" of Joe Barboza was, and remains—regardless of how deeply you're involved, the government has the machinery and the will to help you make a new life for yourself if you will provide evidence of value against organized crime.

So many hoods read the lesson accurately that federal marshal John Partington, the man Barboza so admired, became a specialist in protecting witnesses. A federal official estimated that as of the end of 1973, Partington had more than four hundred such witnesses is his care. All, after their usefulness to the government is ended, will be given a chance to put their pasts behind them and make a new life under a new name.

Aside from such obvious lures as revenge and ultimate freedom, the deals now offered gangsters have a special attraction—the opportunity to be with one's family during the months and years freedom is being earned. It has a practical aspect—the government decided it was just too expensive to protect a witness's family if the family was scattered. By putting all the eggs in one basket, so to speak, it was not only easier to protect them but cheaper. And a lot happier for all concerned.

Perhaps the first to profit by Barboza's example was John "Red" Kelly. A veteran of thirty years, Kelly was indicted in December, 1968, for the armed robbery of a Brinks armored truck. The loot was $542,000 and Kelly was somewhat unhappy at losing a chance to spend his share. The same deal offered Barboza was offered Kelly, and he grabbed it.

Ironically, his story set free the only man convicted until then in Rhode Island in an organized crime case. The man was innocent. Kelly's testimony convicted the real killer and, as a by-product, brought a new ten year sentence to Patriarca for conspiracy in the murder.

Next to follow Barboza was Robert Daddeico, a veteran robber. And his testimony was attuned to the demands of public opinion. The bombing of John Fitzgerald's car had stirred Boston as nothing else, and had served to focus indignation on lawless conditions existing in the Hub City. Daddeico fingered three men—and for Joe Barboza it was the greatest shock of all. The men named were Stevie Flemmi, brother of his beloved Bear, Frank Salanni, a long-time associate of Barboza and Peter Paulos, another associate. That these old friends would forget their loyalty and sell out to the Office—that's how Barboza saw it—was the final disillusionment for a man who had repeatedly risked his life in the gang war for his friends.

The men were indicted, but vanished before they could be arrested. Months later Paulos was found dead in his car in the desert near Las Vegas. Federal officials concluded he was the weak link and had been eliminated by his fellow fugitives.

The FBI spread a net for the missing men and was partly successful. Shortly after Special Agent John Connelly, a native of South Boston, was given a picture, he recognized Salanni on the streets of New York and arrested him. Salanni was convicted; the hunt goes on for Flemmi.

Encouraged by the treatment given Kelly and Daddeico, a parade of mobsters beat their way to Justice Department offices in Boston. And soon the more astute among the FBI agents and the prosecutors recognized a new danger. To win the "Barboza Treatment" a hood had, of course, to sell something of value. The bigger the name the peddlar could drop, the more value it had. But there was only one Patriarca, and he had been twice fingered. So the temptation to exaggerate, to lie, became a factor to reckon with. As one federal official put it: "A hood may tell us a true story except for one thing. The key man may be just another punk so the hood will substitute a big name for the punk. Otherwise the story is true. The only way to guard against the danger is to check out every detail."

Yet for ambitious prosecutors and overworked investigators there is also a temptation to accept the informer's word without checking too closely. A gangster is a gangster, and what does it matter if he gets what's coming to him for the wrong reason? Who will know or care? So goes the logic, and, unfortunately, it is a brand of logic that became increasingly popular during the years when John Mitchell was attorney general of the United States.

An illustration of the conditions existing in a Justice Department avowedly dedicated to "law and order," but in reality more concerned with politics, was supplied by a federal judge in Miami on March 23, 1973. At issue were cases growing out of "Operation Eagle"—the smashing of a massive cocaine distributorship. Judge William Mehrtens threw out the cases on the grounds that essential wiretaps were obtained by "a procedure which included ghost-written, false and misleading memoranda and letters."

The judge noted that similar data submitted by private individuals would have brought contempt of court citations. He added: "This court is not unmindful of the worthwhile law enforcement objectives which are thereby frustrated; however, we are a nation of laws, and if we are to continue to be so, the laws which define and limit the legitimate enterprise of Government within the scope of precious constitutional protections must be enforced with a vigor no less relenting than are those laws which define and limit the legitimate enterprise of individual citizens."

Mitchell's excuse that he had been too busy to attend to details and had delegated his powers to others had a familiar ring in the Year of Watergate, but it convinced few observers who had long been certain that the Nixon administration was more concerned with the appearance of fighting crime than with actual results. Indictments make big news, get a lot of attention, and who remembers when months or years later the case is tossed out of court?

Whether or not one accepts Barboza's version of political throat-cutting in the months he was a federal witness, it is clear that the war on crime in the Boston area degenerated somewhat after Mitchell became attorney general. One of the chief witnesses to agree to testify during that period was Vincent Teresa.

The 300-pound Teresa, formerly Henry Tameleo's chauffeur, suddenly was heralded as "the number three man in the Boston Mafia" after he had been given five years in federal court for stock fraud. In reality, he was no more a member of the Mafia than was Barboza. This did not prevent him from co-authoring a book, *My Life In The Mafia*. Nor did it prevent federal officials from using him to try to convict the biggest gangster of them all—Meyer Lansky, who wasn't a member of the Mafia either.

With a suitable roll of drums the indictment of Lansky on income-tax charges was announced. Lansky, at the time, was in Israel and intended to stay there. It is possible that no one expected to bring the "Little Guy" to trial on the charge. Nevertheless, various events combined to give Lansky unexpected publicity and, after much delay, forced Israel to order him expelled. The reputed financial wizard of crime was given an option as to when he wanted to leave. Interestingly enough, he made a headline-grabbing odyssey across four continents and surrendered in Miami to a squad of FBI agents just forty minutes before the polls opened on Election Day, 1972.

Richard Nixon, for whom Mitchell said he was ready to do almost anything to re-elect, was re-elected, and in July,

1973, Lansky came to trial in Miami. The principal witness, almost the only witness, was Teresa.

The heart of the case involved junkets from Boston to the Colony Club in London. Teresa claimed to be a collector of "markers"—gambling debts from the suckers who were flown to the British gambling joint. Interestingly enough, according to the testimony, the money was divided in this way: Five percent to the Esquire Sporting Club, the collection agency and junket-arranger; five percent to Carlo Mastrototaro, said to be the Mafia boss of Worcester, Mass.; five percent to be divided by Henry Tameleo and Raymond Patriarca; and eighty-five percent to Lansky in Miami.

To those devoted to the legends of La Cosa Nostra, the division didn't make much sense.

Even so, according to the Justice Department, Teresa on occasion delivered Lansky's share to him in person and Lansky, alas, neglected to pay taxes on the income.

The entire case rested then in Teresa's chubby fingers so it is somewhat surprising that the government should have introduced a deposition which pictured their star witness as "an obnoxious glutton who stole chips from the crap tables of a London gambling house."

The deposition described Teresa as "a huge fat man who gobbled enough of the Colony's free food to feed four people and who repeatedly grabbed fistfuls of cigars. He was very objectionable."

Teresa didn't project a better image when he appeared on the stand. He admitted to being a "thief and a hustler since I was twelve years old." He proceeded to tell how in the latter part of May, 1968, he journeyed to Miami and personally delivered some $35,000 to Lansky as his share of the latest junket to London.

Other witnesses proved routinely that Lansky did not report any such sum on his income-tax returns, and the government rested its case.

Lansky's attorney, E. David Rosen, countered quickly by producing records and witnesses to prove that Lansky was in Boston recovering from a double hernia operation at the time Teresa was allegedly giving him cash in Miami.

Obviously, in the rush to indict, someone had failed to check out Lansky's whereabouts at the time the cash was allegedly transferred. This failure was all the more startling in that for years Lansky's every move had been chronicled by government agents on a day-to-day basis.

The jury took less than four hours to acquit Lansky. Jurors told reporters after the trial that they simply didn't believe Teresa, and without Teresa's testimony there was no case.

The fact that Teresa had testified in nineteen previous cases for the government led some observers to wonder how many gangsters he had sent to prison on false testimony. Some federal agents not involved in the Lansky case speculated that Teresa had told the truth up to the point of substituting Lansky's name for a lieutenant who actually took the cash. But indicting the lieutenant wouldn't have made headlines.

That gangsters have been encouraged to perjure themselves in an effort to convict other gangsters may not alarm many, but a parallel can be drawn with the days when informers lied for Senator Joe McCarthy in the battle against "Godless Communism." Under Mitchell, as under McCarthy, a class of professional witnesses was cultivated whose members would point the finger at anyone it was considered desirable to smear. It is a short step from trying to convict a Lansky on perjured testimony for political reasons to using perjured testimony against an opposition candidate. The illegal bugging of Patriarca and scores of other gangsters preceded the attempt to bug the Democratic National Committee in the Watergate Office Building.

All of which doesn't detract from the contribution made by Barboza, by Kelly, by Daddeico and scores of others who risked their lives to tell inside stories about the leaders of organized crime. There is nothing wrong with the system if only it is administered by good men dedicated first to the truth. Such men will take the proper precautions to make sure their witness sticks to the facts, and they will instantly reject a witness who takes liberties. It is unfortunate that the average citizen can't tell the difference between a Barboza and a Teresa except in the courtroom. If a man "looks" like a gangster, "talks" like a gangster, and "boasts" of actions like a gangster, he is usually accepted at face value. Indeed, the staffs of certain Congressional committees are reported to be more concerned with their crime witnesses' appearances than they are with the accuracy of their testimony. Teresa was a big hit before the same committee that made Joe Valachi a household name ten years before. But Valachi was never asked to testify against a Meyer Lanky or a Raymond Patriarca. His legend endures.

We leave now the discussion of Joe Barboza's impact upon society and return to the man.

Happy endings in a history of crime can be achieved only by making an arbitrary decision to halt the narrative at one of those all too infrequent intervals when everything is coming up aces.

Such a point was reached in the preceding chapter when Joe Barboza was given a new identity, job training and a new location where, hopefully, he and his family could make a new life and live happily ever after. To stop at that point would be artistically satisfying and might please sentimental readers who believe rather wistfully that virtue still triumphs sometimes. The more cynical, however, might wonder if a wild animal can be so easily domesticated. Man-eating tigers don't become housepets over night and a Barboza doesn't trade his M-1 rifle for a spatula without encountering adjustment problems. Few men can at age 36 put their past completely behind them, especially when powerful forces from that past still seek to use them. Consequently, albeit reluctantly, it is necessary to scrap the happy ending and admit the saga of Joseph Barboza continued long after his plane flew off into the sunset.

As described, Joe did study cooking at a school on Porter Creek Road in Santa Rosa, California, and he did ship out on a liner to Kowloon, China. While docked at Kowloon, he hurt his back in a shipboard accident. Abruptly his career as a cook came to an end. It had not been unprofitable, however. As compensation for his work-related injury, he received $18,500, and so returned to his family in Santa Rosa with money in his pocket.

With time on his hands it was perhaps inevitable that Joe should become involved with women who, in turn, were mixed up with assorted punks, junkies, con-men and the like. He had, after all, known no other type of person since his youth. It was also inevitable that such associations would lead to trouble.

Before anything developed, however, Barboza received a request to meet with the attorney general of Rhode Island who was interested in developing state charges against Patriarca. After what Joe had heard about Herbert DeSimone, he wasn't sure "I could trust him for the bread"—that is, the expense money. However, since he wanted to contact some of his old friends anyway, Barboza flew to Rhode Island dressed as a hippie: long-haired wig, false beard, beads around his neck, phony glasses, dungarees and boots. As an act of bravado he drove by Patriarca's "Office" in a cab, but he didn't stop to see who was running the store. With some satisfaction he has described the sensation he caused when he appeared at the federal marshal's office in disguise. A conference followed at the headquarters of the Rhode Island State Police—Barboza trusted Colonel Walter Stone—but it achieved nothing of real value. Barboza testified before a Rhode Island grand jury and Patriarca was indicted, but the case never came to trial. In December, 1973, Superior Court Judge Eugene G. Gallant gave Patriarca an early Christmas present by dismissing all of the charges on the grounds that the erstwhile Mafia boss had not received a speedy trial. The dismissal paved the way for a parole bid by Patriarca in 1974. The official excuse for not giving Patriarca a speedy trial was the fact that Barboza was "unavailable." *The Providence Journal* noted, however, that Barboza "never was pleased by the treatment accorded him by members of the attorney general's staff here when he was testifying."

After testifying, Barboza took advantage of his presence in New England to contact an old friend from New Bedford who had the ear of the Office. In so doing he was, he insists, simply trying to buy protection for his wife and children who planned a visit to relatives in Boston. If the Office thought he was willing to recant his testimony, so went his reasoning, it wouldn't bother his family.

Logical; but federal officials close to Barboza think much more was involved. The loss of that $82,000 in bail money when Tashi and DiPrisco were killed at the Nite Lite still rankled. His plan, say these officials, was to promise to retract in exchange for as much as $500,000. With the money in hand or, at least, as much as he could get in advance, he would tell the Mafia to go to hell and leave the country. Originally, the government had planned to send Joe to Australia instead of California. He had balked upon learning he couldn't take his pet dogs. Now, however, he was prepared to go if he could add financial security to the freedom he had already won.

To advance his scheme, Barboza made several trips from California to Boston in the next few months. On occasion he wore an Afro wig and put black pigment on his body. Becoming bolder, he even visited some of the better known joints such as the Attic. All of which was doubly dangerous—

if the Mafia recognized him he was in trouble and if the police spotted him they could arrest him for violating his parole. But the message had gone through to the Office and the process of negotiating was complicated and slow.

A man named Davis was designated to speak for Patriarca and a meet was arranged in some woods near New Bedford. Davis was picked up by one of Barboza's men and brought to the woods. According to Joe, "the woods and the road leading to the woods were staked out with my men." Also present was a Boston reporter who had taken on the task of writing Barboza's history. He was soon to change his mind— allegedly because of pressure from the Mafia.

Just to sweeten the pot a little, Barboza introduced a new element. One of his new friends in California had some $300,000 in stolen stocks and bonds. He had asked Joe to help sell them, so ever-ready Joe offered them to Davis along with his promise to refute his testimony in the Deegan and Marfeo murders. The stocks were to be handled on a straight commission deal. For the rest, Barboza asked for $500,000, plus $1,000 a month while the deal was being worked out. Davis offered $100,000 plus all the money still owed Joe by his shylock customers. In addition, he said, Barboza could have any lawyer in the country at no cost to him. Famed Boston attorney F. Lee Bailey was agreed upon.

This account has been vouched for by reliable federal officials. They also noted that Bailey took the case under the mistaken assumption that Barboza had testified under a grant of immunity and could, therefore, safely confess to having perjured himself in the earlier trials. When Bailey learned otherwise, he withdrew.

Pending a decision on the amount of the bribe, Barboza returned to Santa Rosa where his involvement with various "speed freaks," as he called them, was becoming complicated. Once again it was the same amoral society he had known in Massachusetts—men and women who shifted alliances with equal ease and whose single passion was the pursuit of the fast buck. To them, Barboza was a somewhat mysterious figure from the East. The women found him romantic; the men sought to exploit his shadowy connections with the big wheels of the Mafia. All in all, the general image he projected was favorable until the day he lost his address book.

The address book had FBI phone numbers in Boston, San Francisco and Santa Rosa, Justice Department numbers in Washington, and the numbers of various federal marshals around the country who had served as his guards. He used it to call his contact with the Mafia in Boston from a lounge in Santa Rosa, and dropped it there. Next morning, when he found it missing, he traced it back to the lounge. Everyone looked at him queerly but no one would admit seeing the little book at the Mirror Man. That night, however, some of his friends called him in, showed him the book, and demanded an explanation for all the "pig" numbers it contained.

Barboza gave an explanation which left his image as a tough "Wise Guy" unharmed. His new friends accepted it, or seemed to, but the FBI told him he'd have to move to a new location. Joe agreed, but stalled. He was still hoping to sell the stolen bonds and collect a whopping commission.

All seemed to have settled down when, one day, the current owner of the stocks and bonds asked him to help dig up some guns he had hidden in a woods. Barboza, who was hoping to trade some of his own guns, agreed. Two girls accompanied them—Dee and Paulette. Here is Barboza's account of what happened:

> When we got to the end of a side street called Wake Robin, we drove in a wagon path about fifty feet inside the woods. Clay and I walked ahead of the girls. We were out of their vision because of the darkness. Clay stopped and said: "Listen, you're a fucking snitch. I heard about those guys you put on death row back

east. You can get me for conspiracy because of those stocks."

I said: "If you believe that you deserve anything that happens to you."

I saw Clay's right shoulder go up and his hand go for a gun in his waistband. I wrapped my right arm around his back, grabbing his right elbow with my left. I leaned forward and a shot went off. I felt a tug at my coat. Now I held his right wrist with my left hand. He was six feet, two inches tall, but only weighed 138 pounds. I tripped his legs with a judo move and he fell, with me still holding his wrists. I got the gun out of his hand and was crouched over him with his gun pointed at him. He was swearing and reaching for the small gun he carried in his boot. When his hand reached inside his boot it dawned on me what he was doing. I shot him twice. Later on I found that one bullet went through his eye and the other through his temple.

Straightening up, I searched my body for a bullet hole. There was none. I told the girls who had arrived on the scene to get out. I was wondering if they had lagged behind because they knew Clay was going to try to kill me. The girls left in the car. I dragged the body into the bushes. What the hell was I going to do? The publicity would blow my cover even if the law believed my story. I told myself to think.

I started walking back to the house. Along the way I wiped Clay's gun free of fingerprints and threw the bullets from it in one direction and the gun in another. I emptied the little gun from his boot and put it in my pocket. When I got back to the house the girls were sitting on the porch. Dee said: "Peace, Joe."

I said: "Peace? Did you see what happened up there? Did you know he was going to try it?"

Dee said: "No, Joe, we didn't." Then she said: "Joe, we've got to bury him and avoid the publicity. You can keep the stocks."

I sat there on the porch shocked. This cold-blooded bitch! I had seen her high on drugs and I'd seen her pick a lock and I had heard her and Clay brag about how they had burglarized places together. She sure had a cold heart. But, I thought, it's better for me that she wants to bury him. I won't have to blow my cover and I don't have to take a chance on the law believing me. But what about this 18-year-old snitch, Paulette? Dee seemed to read my mind. She said: "Paulette and I will help you bury him."

Paulette said: "I always hated the punk."

So I agreed and we decided to wait until later in the night when the cars were off the roads. While we were waiting, Paulette and I went back and got the body and put it in the trunk of Clay's car. Dee said she knew where there was some soft ground. Around 4 A.M. we drove off with me in the back seat. We went about twenty-five miles to this private estate which had a road running into it. Dee held the flashlight while I dug. I got down about three feet and the shovel broke. We gave up on that location and drove back to the house. After it began to get light we drove down the road near the spot where I shot Clay. Dee left us to dig and went back for the body. The hole wasn't ready yet when she came back and we made her wait ten minutes. The hole was at the bottom of a cliff. Paulette said she'd help me when my back started hurting. I tied a rope around Clay's feet and Paulette pulled him to the edge of the cliff and I pushed him over and into the hole. We covered up the hole and threw the shovel into the bushes.

When I got home about 7 A.M., my wife was mad at me for staying out all night.

No one seemed to miss Clay very much and by the time Barboza returned to Boston in July, 1970, he was no longer worried about the killing. Negotiations were progressing nicely when trouble of another sort overtook him. Racial violence flared in New Bedford and police declared a curfew. Tensions were high. During a meet on the Fairhaven Bridge, a car full of blacks came along. Words were exchanged. Barboza ended the debate by pointing a .45 automatic at the men. They departed in a hurry and reported the gun-toter to police. A few minutes later Barboza was stopped and arrested. The charge was soon dismissed but the judge held that Barboza had violated his parole. Once again he was returned to Walpole.

Negotiations now broke down between Barboza and the Mafia. A friend to whom Barboza had confided the Clay killing leaked the information to Joe's enemies who quickly passed it on to authorities. Back in Santa Rosa the shallow grave in which Clay was buried was uncovered. The two girls turned state's evidence, and Barboza was indicted for murder.

Eventually the case came to trial. Federal officials who had sought to protect Barboza from himself went out to Santa Rosa and testified about his service to the nation. The local press had a holiday, describing the defendant as an "enforcer for East Coast Mafia." Near the end of the trial the prosecutor offered a deal—first degree murder charges would be dropped if he would plead guilty to second degree murder. Barboza accepted, only to learn later that a number of jurors were convinced of his innocence. Had the case gone to them, they reported, he would have ended up with a hung jury at worst and perhaps acquittal.

Barboza was given a sentence of from five years to life in prison. At the time of this writing he is still serving it. Understandably, he is bitter. Recently he wrote: "I couldn't win on a legitimate self-defense plea because I had formerly associated with the Mafia. You might say, 'Well, he got away with other things so let him take this.' Well, what did I get away with? I paid for my past. The Mafia got me in the end. I've lost my wife and children and that is my biggest sorrow. But I look myself in the face in the mirror and I know I've been right in standing up for what I believe. I've never run away or been frightened."

A brief vacation from prison occurred in May, 1972, when the House Crime Committee starred "Joseph 'the Baron' Barboza" at a hearing in Washington. Wearing dark glasses and a black mustache, Joe looked the part but he was asked to testify largely about things of which he had only hearsay knowledge. Among those things were allegations that Frank Sinatra fronted for Patriarca in the ownership of the Sands in Las Vegas and the Fontainebleau in Miami Beach.

It was a lot of nonsense but the testimony caused a brief sensation and gave Sinatra an excuse to castigate the committee which could have asked more intelligent questions. The committee under the bumbling leadership of Representative Claude Pepper of Florida was desperately seeking sufficient publicity to warrant continuing its existence. The effort failed and the committee died. Barboza, meanwhile, because of his testimony, was quietly transferred to another prison in another state for his better protection.

There he came to terms with himself. As he put it: "The Mafia laughs at me being in prison, but I laugh even louder because I'm still way, way ahead and they can never get even. Never."

Editor's Note

Joe Barboza was paroled in late 1975. On February 11, 1976, he was gunned down and killed on the street in San Francisco. Jerry Anguilo, who had taken control of the New England "Office" after Patriarca's imprisonment, ordered the execution.